Left and Found

Left and Found

Memories Remembered and Told

Patricia LeRoy

Kingdom Living Publishing
Accokeek, MD 20607

Published by:

Kingdom Living Publishing
P.O. Box 660
Accokeek, MD 20607

Published in the United States of America.

ISBN 978-0-9799798-8-0

Dedication

In loving memory of my sister Gertrude (Gertie) who welcomed me with open arms and shared so much about our family with me. You will always be a special sister. I miss you and love you dearly.

Also in loving memory of my son Joey. Without his love for his mother and help, I could not have written this book. I miss you and love you so very much.

Acknowledgments

I would like to give special thanks to all my children Mickie Goss, Beth Goss Robb, Joey Goss (deceased), Kevin LeRoy, Lucinda LeRoy Glaug, Shannon LeRoy, and Doricia LeRoy Benton for helping and encouraging me to write my book.

I would like to thank all of my friends for caring about me during my long journey and quest to find my sister.

I would like to thank my publisher, Irma McKnight for publishing "Left and Found" and for her patience and kindness throughout this process.

Table of Contents

Chapter One

A Unique Story

While we were living in Wichita, Kansas, in 1967, I had a wild impulse. I grabbed the phone and dialed the long distance operator. It was a call I had fought myself from making for thirty-five years. I could hold back no longer. Suddenly I was overwhelmed with feelings of anxiety, fear, and even excitement. Did I really dare to make this call? Just as I was about to put the receiver back, the friendly voice of the operator was saying, "Long distance operator. May I help you, please?" "Yes, thank you, I would like to place a call," I answered. "To whom would you like to place a call," she asked. Now what I had been dreading was happening. I did not honestly know whom I was trying to call. "Operator, may I explain whom I am and who I am trying to locate?" Then I held my breath and waited for her answer. Telephone operators are so busy; I was afraid she might turn me down after I had finally gotten enough "courage" to call. Almost immediately, she answered, "Please explain. I'll be glad to help you if I can." I quickly began explaining whom I was and how very important it was for me to find these special people. "We will give it a try," the operator said." "I wish you the very best in your search." As she plugged in the circuit to make the call to Indianapolis, Indiana, I could hear the code language of the telephone operator. Their voices seemed to fade as stronger thoughts came to my mind. What did I really know about my life? Each of our lives is a unique story, each one interesting, and each one different. I had quite a bit of information to help in my search, even though I had been adopted.

Where did it all begin for me? It all began for me in the year 1932, during the Great Depression, in Shreveport, Louisiana. I was trying to remember everything just as my adopted mama had told me. It was a very cold winter morning when my young mother and father, my biological parents, slipped into the courtroom of the Caddo Parish Courthouse. In their arms, they cradled two young helpless children. Their hearts ached to be able to care for them, but their having no money or job made it impossible. My father stepped quickly but softly up to the judge and asked for a helping hand, not for himself or his wife, but for their children. The judge looked at my father and choked back tears of heartache. As a judge, he had seen so much during the hard years of the depression. In a voice of deep concern and helplessness he said, "I am so sorry; there are not even jobs for the people of our state. You will have to appeal to your own state for help. I am sorry. I am truly sorry."

The disappointment my father felt could not be measured by mere words. The heartache of a man with a wife and two young children and no money or jobs was unbearable. Across the courtroom, his eyes met the tear-stained eyes of his wife. She knew they had been turned down. Now what would they do and where could they turn for help? They were so young with two small children. Patricia, who was called Patsy, was nineteen months old; she had big brown eyes and naturally curly red hair. Tears fell as the young mother ran her fingers through Patsy's curls. She did not understand the tears her mother shed. My mother realized she was leaving and she took off her necklace with a Catholic Medal on it and put it around my neck. This would be the only possession of hers that I would have. I still wear it. Little Michael, seven months old with blond hair and big blue eyes, was sleeping. He never saw the tears nor felt them wet against his pale little face. How unaware little Michael was that he would never see his mommy and daddy again.

Suddenly I heard the operator's voice saying, "Are you still holding the line?" "Yes, I am, operator. Have you located someone for me?" I asked anxiously. "I'm very sorry; no one seems to know the people you are trying to locate. Do you have any more names we can try?" "Well, I was born in Chicago; may we try to locate them there?" I asked hopefully. "We will try again; please hold the line," the operator said as she put through the call to Chicago. I listened for a few minutes; then I started to remember again, where I was. Oh yes, the courtroom.

All of a sudden, the courtroom was very busy. In the hustle and bustle, no one noticed a sad and softly crying mother and father slipping quietly out a side door. The children were asleep, and then they woke up and began to cry. They were alone and afraid. No one was able to find the children's mother and father.

DOWN WAGES

who takes advantage of
rable unemployment situ-
own wages is making a
first place he will find
income of his employees
by his fellow employers.
business man knows that
ges is destructive of mar-
lost job means a lost cus-
urn, means more lost jobs
1ore customers.

| that between 13 and 17
this country are out of
:hat many with their de-
omers with no purchasing

cause of the depression,
ot bring it on nor will low
it. As a matter of fact
h ability to earn the peak
main cog in the wheel of
ns his money in his home
ds it at home. That being
nit this:

workman could stay in
get a job and spend his
ie confines of where he
1't the result bring pros-
own and in turn benefit
ring concern and business
own for trade.

TWO LITTLE BABES

Written for the Plain Dealer.

Two little waifs—neglected—forlorn—
Were left at the Juvenile Court one morn.
    A sweet little girl, a bright little boy—
    A father's delight and a fond mother's joy—
Some say they were better unborn.

No witnesses sworn—no clerk made report—
Just two little babes in the Juvenile Court.
    Two sweet little flowers with blossoms scarce blown—
    Their kinfolk unguessed and their country unknown—
Had chosen to live in Shreveport.

No counsel read briefs of rhetorical phrases—
The crier's singsong was subdued by mute praises
    For these little strangers so trusting and tender—
    Embarked on life's journey and loath to surrender
Though lost in its jungles and mazes.

No statute was cited—no law need embrace—
The judge's decision was wrote on the face
    Of each little tot as it lay in repose—
    Bereft of its parents and shorn of its clothes—
His sentence was some cozy place

In the home of some citizen—noble and true—
Who would teach them respect for that mother none knew,
    Who sacrificed joy on the altar of love.
    Let angels pay tribute from mansions above,
While mortals this spirit imbue.

ly the day girls complained of the strong
odor and being sick. We worked in artificial light all day.
  "We had no provision whatsoever for
our clothes. We had no rest room and no

HAVE "GOT TO DO IT"

It seems to us that the people of
port have had about enough of thi

Someone wrote this poem, "Two Little Babes," about Michael and me. It was published in *The Plain Dealer* newspaper. It is reprinted on the next page for easier reading.

       Left and Found

Two Little Babies

(Written for "The Plain Dealer")

Two little waifs—neglected—forlorn—
Were left at the Juvenile Court one morn.
A sweet little girl, a bright little boy—
A father's delight and a fond mother's joy—
Some say they were better unborn.

So witnesses sworn—no clerk made report—
Just two little babes in the Juvenile Court.
Two sweet little flowers with blossoms scarce blown—
Their kinfolk unguessed and their country unknown.
Had chosen to live in Shreveport.

No counsel read briefs of rhetorical phrases—
The crier's singsong was subdued by mute praises
For these little strangers so trusting and tender—
Embarked on life's journey and loath to surrender
Though lost in its jungles and mazes.

No statute was cited—no law need embrace—
The judge's decision was wrote on the face
Of each little tot as it lay in repose—
Bereft of its parents and shorn of its clothes—
His sentence was some cozy place.

In the home of some citizens—noble and true—
Who would teach them respect for that mother none knew.
Who sacrificed joy on the altar of love,
Let angels pay tribute from mansions above,
While mortals, this spirit imbue.

ABANDONED BABY OF MR. & MRS. E. W. HARPER

"EXHIBIT A "

Patricia Francis Harper was born   in Chicago, Illinois.
Her parents are Earl William Harper and Evelyn McCauley Harper.
These parents had one other child, Michael, born 5/16/1932 in
Washington, D. C. and died 1/2/1933 in Shreveport, Louisiana.
On December 28, 1932, Mr. & Mrs. Harper and their two children
came to the Juvenile Court to ask the Court to take their
children in order that they might have food. They were hungry
and cold, the father was sick, and the mother very frail. The
baby was terribly undernourished but Patricia was in fairly good
physical condition. The parents told a story of having always
lived in Chicago, leaving there in June 1932 in an old car to
come South and look for work. Conditions became worse all the
time and finally, they were forced to ask the Court to take their
children to keep them from starving. The Court was not in favor
of taking these children and when the parents had the opportunity
they slipped out of the Court room, leaving the children. They
have never been heard from since that day.

JUVENILE CASE RECORD

Earl W. Harper children

FAMILY RECORD NO.

PROBATION OFFICER

DATE OF SUMMARY 12/28/3 2

SUMMARY

CHILD'S NAME (SURNAME FIRST)	AGE	ADDRESS
Harper--Patricia and Michael	19 mo. & 7 mo.	Shreveport, La.

SCHEDULE OF TOPICS

1. COMPLAINT: DATE, SOURCE, CAUSE AND CIRCUMSTANCES. STATEMENTS OF CHILD, WITNESSES, PARENTS AND OTHERS.

2. THE HOME: MAKE-UP, HISTORY, ATTITUDE OF FAMILY. HEALTH OF MEMBERS, PHYSICAL AND MENTAL, ALCOHOLISM, DRUG ADDICTION, ETC. CITIZENSHIP DATA, COURT OR POLICE RECORDS. ECONOMIC CONDITION, OCCUPATIONS AND WAGES OF EMPLOYED MEMBERS, TOTAL INCOME, DEBTS, SAVINGS. ARRANGEMENTS FOR CARE OF CHILDREN IF MOTHER EMPLOYED. PHYSICAL CONDITION OF HOME, SANITATION, OVER-CROWDING, STANDARD OF LIVING, ROOMERS. CHARACTER OF NEIGHBORHOOD.

3. THE CHILD: EARLY LIFE, DEVELOPMENT, TRAINING, PERSONALITY, HABITS, CONDUCT, POSITION IN THE HOME, DELINQUENCY AND INSTITU- TIONAL RECORD. PHYSICAL AND MENTAL CONDITION. REPORT OF EXAMINATIONS IF ANY. SCHOOL HISTORY, SCHOLARSHIP, ATTENDANCE, CONDUCT. EMPLOYMENT HISTORY. RECREATION, COMPANIONS, INTERESTS, RELIGIOUS LIFE.

4. AGENCIES: SOCIAL AGENCIES, INSTITUTIONS AND INDIVIDUALS INTERESTED IN THE FAMILY. KIND OF SERVICE RENDERED, SUMMARY OF RECORD.

5. RECOMMENDATIONS AND PLAN.

Mr. & Mrs. Harper and two babies came to the office to ask that the Juvenile Court take the children into the Detention Home as they were sick and hungry and they were unable to give them the proper care. Mr. Harper said they had spent the last three weeks in Minden, La. The Red Cross in Minden had given them a place to stay with a family named Welch. They stayed there until the baby became very ill with ear trouble and the Red Cross sent them on to Shreveport in order that the child could go to Charity Hospital. He said the Red Cross had told them to continue on their way as soon as the child was able to travel. The baby was a patient in the hospital about two days. The Salvation Army here gave Mr. & Mrs. Harper a bed for one night and told them to move on. Mr. Harper said he was a machinist by trade. He has lived in Chicago all of his life. He left there in June, 1932, coming South to look for work. He left in a Nash car. He has traveled continuously since--staying in Houston three months. He traded his car for an old Ford and came to Minden. This car was left in Minden. He is an ex-service man and had appealed to the American Legion here and every other place for aid. They help him enough to get on to the next town. He insisted that he couldn't continue to take the children as they were starving and he had begged for them until he could do this no longer. Mrs. Harper says her parents are dead--she was an only child, all her parent's relatives live in Ireland. She had no relatives at all who might assist her with the children. Officer explained to them that this Court never accepted children for care who were not residents of Louisiana-- that the Court was not finacially able to care for its own; and that the only exception to this was in cases where children were abandoned. Officer was called from the room for a few minutes and on returning found the children but the parents were gone. They evidently decided to abandon the children in order to save their lives. The babies were taken to the Detention Home. Michael was released the same day to Mr. Clint Sanders who took him to his home for temporary care. Patricia was released to a Mr. & Mrs. Jouett for temporary care. Dr. Worley was called to see Michael-- he says the child has rickets(caused from malnutrition), has had a bad time with both ears, and is so badly undernourished it is hard to tell just what the outcome will be. Patricia is also undernourished but is in better physical condition than the baby.

Child and Probation Association - 130 Seventh Ave. New York, N. Y.

(Continue on reverse and on plain sheets)

ILLINOIS EMERGENCY RELIEF COMMISSION
RELIEF ADMINISTRATION—COOK COUNTY
LEO M. LYONS, ADMINISTRATOR

November 19, 1934

UNEMPLOYMENT RELIEF SERVICE
UNION PARK DISTRICT
25 SOUTH SEELEY AVENUE
TELEPHONE SEELEY 7121
MRS. ANNA DALTON JOYCE, SUPERVISOR

RE: HARPER, Earl & Evelyn,
1310 Van Buren Street.
Child: Gertrude,

RECEIVED
NOV 26 1934

REFER TO

State Emergency Relief Administration,
708 Canal Bank Building,
New Orleans, Louisiana.

Gentlemen:

Will you please clear with your Social Service Exchange
and ask for summaries of the contacts of any organization
in your city with the Harper family?

Mr. and Mrs. Harper who are applying to our organization
for assistance, advise us that late in 1932 and in the
early part of 1933, they visited Shreveport with their
two children, Michael and Patricia. Michael died in
December and Patricia was taken away from the family by
the Juvenile Court. Mr. Harper states that Mrs. Truly,
was the probation officer.

We thank you very much for your co-operation in this
matter.

Yours very truly,

UNEMPLOYMENT RELIEF SERVICE

Kathleen Bellmore
(Mrs.) Kathleen Bellmore,
District Supervisor.

WILLIS:ED

Nine cents in stamps
is enclosed to cover
cost of forwarding to
the proper authority.

December 3, 1934

Unemployment Relief Service
Union Park District
25 South Seeley Avenue
Chicago, Ill.

        Attention: Mrs. Kathleen Bellmore

        In re: Patricia and Michael Harper 33 63

Dear Mrs. Bellmore:

        Your letter addressed to the State E. R. A., in New
Orleans, was forwarded to this office for reply.

        According to our records, Patricia Frances Harper was
born   in Chicago, Illinois. Her parents are
Earl William Harper and Evelyn McCauley Harper. These
parents had one other child, Michael, born May 16, 1932, in
Washington, D. C., and died January 2, 1933, in Shreveport,
Louisiana.

        On December 28, 1932, Mr. and Mrs. Harper and their two
children came to the Juvenile Court in Shreveport to ask the
Court to take their children in order to keep them from starvation. The father was sick at the time and the mother was
very frail. The baby was very sick, having spent sometime
in the Charity Hospital here, but Patricia appeared to be
in fairly good physical condition.

        The parents told a story of having always lived in
Chicago, leaving there in June, 1932, in an old car to come
South and look for work. The parents abandoned their children
in the Court room here and this is the first time that we have
had any hearing from them.

        After the baby died, the Court kept Patricia until
August 23, 1933, hoping that the parents would return or
that some hearing would be had from them. At that time, the
little girl was placed for adoption and under the Louisiana
law, a period of four months must elapse before the adoption
is completed. At the end of that time, the child had been in

A Unique Story   19

the care of the Court a whole year and the parents had never
been heard from. The adoption was completed and it is against
the law for the Court to give out any information in regard to
the adoption.

I notice from your letter that the Harpers have another
child. I might add that a great deal of newspaper publicity
was given this case over a long period of time in the hopes
that the mother and father would have knowledge of the death
of their child and that conditions would improve with them
and they would be moved to come back to Shreveport for their
little girl.

The little girl is receiving the very best of care and
I hope that the Harpers have no intention of making any effort
to regain possession of the child, because it would be a matter
of impossibility.

Sincerely yours,

Mrs. R. E. Truly

T/M

Chapter Two

Homes for Baby Michael and Patricia

A cub newspaper reporter, Clint Sanders, was at Court that day for the local court news. He heard the children crying and walked over to see if he could help. There was a note pinned to Michael's blanket. It read, "We understand you can't help us, but please help our two helpless babies. Thank you." The Judge had told my father they could only help the children if they were abandoned. The reporter was so touched with compassion for little Michael that he wanted to adopt him. He asked someone to take a picture of him holding Michael. That newspaper picture is the only picture I have of Michael. The Judge granted him permission to take baby Michael home with him. Michael was very weak and sick, hardly able to cry. Right away, the reporter took Michael to the hospital; there he received the best medical care available. The next morning the picture of Clint Sanders holding Michael appeared in the newspaper along with the story.

People everywhere responded to the story. It touched their hearts; Clint Sanders even received proposals of marriage. Poor baby Michael. The months of hardship, malnutrition, and exposure had taken their toll on him. He was too weak to rally; his chance in life had come too late and Michael slipped away quietly in death to be with God and His angels. Clint Sanders and his family went to the funeral for Michael. Cook Brothers Funeral Home took care of the funeral. The Reverend Wynn spoke comforting words on the subject, *"Suffer the Little Children to Come unto Me."* Then little Michael was laid to rest in "Babyland" in Greenwood Cemetery in Shreveport, Louisiana. I was taken to Juvenile Children's Home where I was given good care. However, I did not understand where my mama and daddy were or where my little brother Michael was. Fate was much kinder to me than it was to little Michael.

A grocer and his wife, Joseph and Elizabeth Jouett, had no children, but they had wanted some very much. They were very good to Juvenile Children's Home and often brought groceries and fruit to the children and staff. Late one evening the phone rang at the Jouett's home. When they answered, they never dreamed of the news that they were about to hear. It was the Juvenile Home, and officials wanted them to come see a little girl with curly red hair and brown eyes. Her name was Patsy; she was nineteen months old, and she needed a home. The woman went on to explain that Patsy and her little brother Michael, seven months old, had been abandoned by their desperate parents. "We will be right over," replied my adopted mama. It was only a few minutes until they were knocking at the door of Juvenile Children's Home. When they saw Patsy, tears came to their eyes and their hearts filled with love for the little girl. They took her home with them. Her bed was the front porch swing and her bottle was a coke bottle with a nipple. In those days to love a child was reason enough to adopt him or her. Soon Joseph and Elizabeth Jouett were making inquiries about a legal and formal adoption of Patsy. The same Judge, Judge Fullilove, who had spoken with my father in the courtroom the day we were abandoned, helped with the adoption papers. Soon Patsy had a new Mama and Daddy. The

Left and Found

adoption gave Patsy a new Grandmother too. She loved little Patsy from the start, and her love was returned by a dear little girl who called her "Granny."

Again, the operator's voice broke into my thoughts. I heard her saying "Are you still there?" Quickly I snapped back to the present. "Yes, I am," I answered, "Were you able to locate anyone who knew anything at all?" "I'm so sorry," she said. "No one knows anything that can help you locate those special people." "What will I do now?" I whispered to myself. Then aloud I said to the operator, "There is one last chance." I have a copy of my birth certificate. Let me check the names on my mother's side. They are from a small town named Harvard in North Eastern Indiana. Please, may we try just one more time?"

Right away, the operator began to put through the call. At this point, I felt the operator really wanted to help me. Again I was waiting with the hope of any little bit of news. Then the operator's voice came through loud and clear. She was saying, "I have some news for you; one lady I spoke with said she did not know anything herself, but she remembered her husband talking about it years ago. She said when her husband returned from work she would ask him and have him return your call." The operator went on to say," I gave her your name and phone number, I am so happy for you. I hope everything will be fine, for you. Thank you for letting me help you in my own small way." I was in tears as I thanked the operator. I did not even know her name, but I knew I would never forget her. My hopes were so high and I was excited as I waited for the woman in Indiana to call me. While I was waiting by the phone for her call, more thoughts were rushing through my mind about the endless questions I would ask her. Oh my, the sheer excitement of just knowing something after all these years of searching; it was almost too much! I wondered if my pounding heart could take it. I know my heart and my mind. I know I yearned to know my real mother and father. I truly understood how it was during the depression, and I understand how it was that they abandoned Michael and me. Because they loved us but had no money or any way to care for us, they felt their only choice was to leave us at the mercy of the court. They knew to leave us would give us a chance for life. How very sad to think that even then it was too late for Michael. His chance came too late, as he was very sick; it breaks my heart. Without a doubt, my mother and father's lives were affected by what happened on that day in the courtroom.

I need to say at this point in my story that I talked to my adopted mama several times about trying to find my birth parents. Every time she said, "That will be fine Pat. I understand and I hope you can find them." She never made me feel guilty or that it was not the thing to do because you see, I loved my mama, daddy, and granny with all my heart and they knew this. Therefore, I know they understood how I felt about everything.

The Bible Verse, Romans 8:28, expresses my heart's feelings: *"And we know that all things work together for good to them that love God, to them who are called according to His purpose."* We just have to have faith. All these thoughts were going through my mind as I anxiously waited for a call from a woman that could help me. No one will ever know how much courage it took to pick up the phone, talk to a telephone operator that I did not know nor did she know me, and place those calls to people and places I did not know. Please let her call! If only she knew how much it meant to me. I waited just about the whole day, but no return call. All of my hopes had been in vain. The woman never did call me. For a long time, every time the phone would ring, I would hope. Most days were ordinary days, but some held special memories like these!

Scribe Adopts Baby

Clint Sanders, 24, unmarried Shreveport, La., reporter, has adopted the four months' old baby boy shown in his arms. He found the child deserted in Shreveport juvenile court which is part of his daily "run." (Associated Press Photo)

This newspaper clipping of Clint Sanders and Michael is the only picture there is of Michael Harper.

State of Louisiana

In the interests of the Minor

~~Michael Harper age 7 mos~~

No.___3363___

In the Juvenile Court
of Caddo Parish, La.

JUDGMENT GRANTING CUSTODY

The law and the evidence being in favor thereof.   It is ordered, adjudged and decreed

that the custody of the minor_____Michael ᵇ Harper_____
XXXXXs

_____

be and the same is hereby placed in the custody of_____Mrs W M Sanders_____

_____

whose address is_____616 Stoner, Shreveport, L a._____

Done and signed on this the___29th___day of___December___A. D. 193_2_

_____S C Fullilove_____
                                                                    Judge

A TRUE COPY

Mrs Ruby Cavender
_____
                        Clerk of Court

Long Period Without Food Causes Death of Babe Here

Seven-Month-Old Child Deserted Here by Parents and Cared For by Newspaperman Unable to Rally From Exposure.

Death came to little Michael Harper Tuesday just as life began to bloom in his sad little life. This 7-month-old tot who had known hunger, cold, privation and disease, died just as he had gained what he needed most—a home, food and had seen life at its worst. First he had proper care.

Despite his tender age, Michael was homeless, then hungry, then cold and finally abandoned. The rigors of such a life were too much for one of his tender age and despite efforts of doctors and those who had taken charge of this little waif, he died Tuesday, a victim of malnutrition and exposure. His chance in life came too late.

Little Michael came into Shreveport Dec. 28 in the arms of his penniless and distressed parents, who were unable to provide him and his 19-month-old sister food that was so greatly needed. The parents, who gave their names as Mr. and Mrs. Earl William Harper of Chicago, were in Shreveport with two hungry children on their hands and not a cent in their pockets and not a friend to appeal to. They decided to go to the juvenile court and there they appealed to the authorities to take their two children, as they were unable to provide them with food.

The little girl was in a tantrum, she was so hungry, and in order to quiet her the father went outside, begged a dime and bought her some cakes. Little Michael was so ill that he was hardly able to utter a cry. While officers of the court were considering the case, little Michael was kept in a small bed made by placing two chairs together. Then something happened. While no one was looking, the parents walked out and left the two children. Efforts to locate them a few minutes later were in vain. But fortune smiled in the case.

In walked Clint Sanders, a Shreveport newspaper reporter. A glance at little Michael moved him to pity. He asked for custody of the child and was given it by Judge S. C. Fullilove. He took the baby to his mother, Mrs. W. M. Sanders, 616 Stoner avenue. A doctor's examination showed the child to be in bad condition. It was suffering from rickets, caused by malnutrition, and its ears were badly affected. The best physicians of the city were called to attend the child and it was taken to a hospital for treatment, but the exposure and lack of food had been too much. Tuesday morning little Michael died.

Where little Michael's father and mother are is not known here. They told attaches at the juvenile court that they were trying to hitch hike their way to Chicago. The couple, according to the authorities appeared to be well bred. Harper said that he was a mechanic who had been out of work for some time. Both shed tears as they told of their pitiful plight and of trying to care for their children.

Incidentally little Michael's 19-month-old sister has been placed in a good home here and is in good physical condition, it was reported

Baby Boy Adopted by Young Reporter Dies at Shreveport

SHREVEPORT, La., Jan. 5—(By A. P.)—There is grief today in the home of Clinton Sanders, 24-year old Shreveport newspaper reporter, because of the death of 7-month-old Michael Harper, foundling.

The child was adopted recently by the reporter after he had seen its pitiful condition in juvenile court. Little Michael and a 29-month-old sister were deserted in the court when the hitch-hiking parents, destitute, were told the tribunal had authority only to care for infants. During the hearing, the parents slipped quietly away, leaving the children on the mercy of the court.

Sanders, unmarried, was present during the proceedings and immediately asked leave to adopt Michael and take him home to his own parents, Mr. and Mrs. W. M. Sanders. The 19-month-old little girl was placed in another home.

Homes for Baby Michael and Patricia

27

A Tribute

To Judge Fullilove.

Thou art gone, our friend,
From this sad world of pain,
And shall we never, never see
Your smiling face again.

Yes, God has called you home,
Up to heaven to Him.
The angels gently bore you
Far through the ether dim.

And then they gently laid you
Safe at the Savior's feet,
And left you there as though your
    rest
Had been a breathing sleep.

When we meet we shall miss you,
We shall see your vacant chair;
How often we will think of you,
When we breathe our evening
    prayer.

And when our time shall come
And we are called to go,
We hope to meet and greet you,
On heaven's beautiful shore.

Editor's Note.

These are the sentiments of
Judge Fullilove's juveniles as ex-
pressed by a friend.

Laws of Hunger Win Out Over Laws of Man Here

Undernourished Children of Michigan Couple Deserted by Parents so That Statutes May Be Set Aside

A Michigan couple, whose two infant, undernourished children were
not legally entitled to receive the care
and attention of the Caddo parish
juvenile court, made certain Wednesday that laws of man would not
deprive the tots of a livelihood. They
carried both children to the reception
room of the court and abandoned
them.

Found by Judge S. C. Fullilove and
members of his staff, the two youngsters, one a boy of seven months and
the other a girl of 19 months, were
sent immediately to the juvenile detention home, where the blonde
youngsters remained for less than five
hours before two families asked to
adopt them.

Laws under which the court func-
tions do not permit it to make wards
of children whose parents do not live
within its jurisdiction. Abandoned
children are exceptions and can be
cared for by the court.

(Continued On Page Eleven.)

Undernourished Child, Deserted by Parents, Dies in Hospital Here

Jan 3 1933

7-Months-Old Michael Harper, Left in Juvenile Courtroom by Destitute Parents, Succumbs to Starvation

Under-nourishment and illness
triumphed Tuesday morning over
care and affection as seven-months-
old Michael Harper, deserted December 28 by his penniless and distressed parents, died in a hospital
here.

Clinton Sanders, a reporter for The
Times, who had taken the child to
his home after seeing its pitiful condition in juvenile court, where it was
abandoned, was not at work Tuesday. This morning he and his parents, Mr. and Mrs. W. M. Sanders,
and the Sanders family, will attend
funeral services at 10 o'clock at Mc-
Cook Brothers Funeral home. The
Rev. J. M. Wynn will speak a few
comforting words in the subject,
"Suffer the little children to come
unto Me", and then the tot will be
placed at rest in Greenwood cemetery.

The child was one of two deserted
in the courtroom, December 28. The
parents had been informed that the
court could not care for the children because the parents did not re-
side in Caddo parish and that it
could care for children without its
jurisdiction only when they had been
abandoned. While court attaches were
busy the parents slipped from the
room.

The young newspaperman, coming
into the court, saw the pitiful condition of the children. Judge Fullilove
allowed him to take Michael home.
The other child, a 19-months-old
girl, was placed in another good
home. Every bit of attention and
medical skill available was showered
upon the child, but his constitution
weakened by starvation, he died.

This morning his parents, probably hitch-hiking southward with
aching hearts, are wondering how
their two children, abandoned because
they had found it impossible to care
for them, are getting along. A light-
haired little girl with blue eyes may
be wondering where her little brother
is. And a preacher will attempt to
say a few comforting words to bereft foster-parents as a small casket
is lowered into the ground.

HUNGER LAWS ARE STRONGER

(Continued From Page One.)

The couple who deserted their
young here Wednesday night had
been residing recently in Houston and
Minden. Their home was in Michigan
but hard times sent them southward
in search of work. Neither child has
had the proper food and clothing for
months and both were almost fam-
ished when found Wednesday, court
attaches said. The mother and father
previously had appeared in person at
the court to ask its help in providing
a living for the children, but Judge
Fullilove, who personally made an
effort to give them something from
his own pocket, was forced to tell
them the parish would not permit ac-
ceptance of children unless deserted.

Cry of Undernourished Baby Echoes 'Round U.S.

Reporter's Action in Adopting Abandoned Child Stirs Wave of Sympathy Across the Nation

The cry of an undernourished baby, which played upon the heartstrings of an unmarried Shreveport newspaper man and caused him to adopt a child, has been heard around the United States. Letters and messages of congratulations are a medium from which to judge.

When Clinton Sanders walked into the juvenile court room last December and saw the helpless babe, deserted by parents who could not support it, he decided something should be done. He phoned his mother, made the arrangements and took the baby home and thought the matter was ended.

But the baby had too much and suffering from several maladies, died several days later, despite the efforts of some of Shreveport's best physicians to keep the tiny spark of life glowing.

After Sanders carried the baby to his home the fact was mentioned, in passing, in "The Stroller" column of this newspaper. An illustrated photographer snapped a picture of Sanders and the baby. The news of the adoption reached the major press wires of the nation and letters began to pour in. People everywhere responded to the story. Its essence was such as to touch the very heartstrings of the American people.

Letters from 17 states in two weeks complimented the reporter, congratulated him and wished him happiness. Most of them were from women.

Several Marriage Proposals

Pictures of Sanders and the baby were published in the Des Moines Tribune, the St. Louis Post-Dispatch, the Memphis Commercial Appeal, the Jackson (Miss.) Clarion-Ledger, the Savannah Morning News, the Hagerstown (Md.) Press, the Denver Post, the Chattanooga Times, the Atlanta Constitution, the Lake Charles (La.) American Press, the New Orleans States, Forth Worth Star-Telegram, the New York Herald-Tribune, the Arkadelphia (Ark.) Herald, the Arkansas Gazette, the El Dorado (Ark.) News and Times, the Philadelphia (Pa.) Bulletin, the University of Indiana Daily Student, the Meridian (Miss.) Star, the Chicago Tribune and numerous other publications affiliated with the Associated Press.

Several of the girls in writing to Sanders made outright proposals of marriage and offered a mother's (they being the mothers) love, care and affection. Many of them sent descriptions of themselves and some enclosed pictures. One of the photographs was of a very pretty girl with large dark eyes, pretty lips and an abundance of dark, wavy hair—a break for any baby. The picture caused several other reporters for themselves for adoption.

Handy on a Farm

One girl living on a rural free delivery route in Ohio emphasized the fact that if Sanders should choose her, they could move to a farm, because she is, she said, doing anything on a farm. Sanders had not left Shreveport late Saturday night.

However, most of the letters adhere to the centenerates' ring of sincerity. Most of the correspondents wrote because the adoption struck a tender chord in their hearts. Some wished just to correspond.

The department of agriculture at Washington, D. C., informed of the adoption by some local wit, mailed Sanders a ton (more or less) of literature on "Hints on Child Care."

Today the baby lies buried in the Greenwood cemetery. Its parents are somewhere along life's highway, but

Its moral seems to be that so long as human beings show human traits and act toward one another as human beings, as in this case, the world is not such a bad place after all.

CANNING PLANT IS PLANNED TO AID D'RIDDER FARMERS

DeRidder, Feb. 25 (Special).—Arrangements for free community canning of vegetables, fruit and meat during the spring, summer and fall seasons are being made by M. L. Cooper, parish agent.

Mr. Cooper plans to have factory equipment and to designate two days each week for the canning, with the various communities allotted their day and time. An expert canner will be present to give instructions and to assist canners. Miss Clyde Schilling, home demonstration agent, is co-operating with Mr. Cooper.

Longview Will Name Commission in April

Longview, Texas, Feb. 25 (Special). Three commissioners will be named at a city election here the first Tuesday in April. The terms of Commissioners J. W. Dalton, L. D. Kelly and G. C. Finch will expire this spring. Dalton is chairman of the commission. Current reports are to the effects that all three of the retiring commissioners will have opponents should they aspire to re-election.

LOUISIANA STATE BOARD OF HEALTH,
Bureau of Vital Statistics
CERTIFICATE OF DEATH

1—PLACE OF DEATH

Parish ... Caddo
Ward ... 4
City or Town ... Shreveport, La.

Registered No. 166

No. Shreveport Charity Hospital

2—FULL NAME ... Mickel Harper

(a) Residence. No. 616 Stoner Ave., Shreveport, La. Ward.

PERSONAL AND STATISTICAL PARTICULARS

3. SEX — Male
4. COLOR OR RACE — White
5. SINGLE, MARRIED, WIDOWED, OR DIVORCED — Single

6. DATE OF BIRTH — 1932
7. AGE — 7 Months

8. Trade, profession — None

12. BIRTHPLACE — Unknown / Unknown
13. NAME — Unknown
14. BIRTHPLACE — Unknown / Unknown
15. MAIDEN NAME — Unknown
16. BIRTHPLACE — Unknown / Unknown
17. INFORMANT — M. M. Sanders
616 Stoner Ave., Shreveport, La.
18. BURIAL — Greenwood Cemetery — Jan. 4, 1933
19. UNDERTAKER — McCook Bros. F.H.
Shreveport
20. FILED — 1-3-33

MEDICAL CERTIFICATE OF DEATH

21. DATE OF DEATH — Jan. 3, 1933
22. I HEREBY CERTIFY, That I attended deceased from Jan. 3, 1933 to Jan. 3, 1933

Contributory causes ... Malnutrition

24. (Signed) ... M.D.

MAY 27 1987

I CERTIFY THAT THIS IS A TRUE AND CORRECT COPY OF A CERTIFICATE OR DOCUMENT REGISTERED WITH THE VITAL RECORDS REGISTRY OF THE STATE OF LOUISIANA, PURSUANT TO LSA - R.S. 40:32, ET SEQ.

STATE HEALTH OFFICER   STATE REGISTRAR

30   Left and Found

January 3rd, 1933.

Mrs W M Sanders
616 Stoner
Shreveport, La.

My Dear Mrs Sanders:

No mortal can understand the ways of the Divine One. Here was a little babe, innocent of all sin, pure as Christ himself, condemned to live a life of extreme poverty and hardship. And just when its own innocent helplessness had won it the care, tenderness and love of fine people--just when it got its only chance for relief from those awful conditions, it must pass. But in spite of this, there is a Divine Plan in everything.

Who knows what this little one has done, and will do, for Clint? It certainly aroused his sympathies, and he will always be the better for having done this Christlike act. And possibly you, and other members of your family, will be the better for having given so freely to "one of the least of these little ones".

I know you sorrow in this tragedy. Down here where we contact the flotsam and jetsam of humanity, we appreciate the great battle you fought for the life of this little one, and particularly so, for we know now that it was hopeless from the first. But it is the finest thing that ever came within my knowledge! May not God and his angels (including the little one) rejoice that so much of the divine spark was developed by this little boy?

Please be assured of our appreciation, our sympathy and our love.

Sincerely,

Homes for Baby Michael and Patricia   31

File

Elizabeth, La.,
Feb. 27, 1933

Judge S. C. Fullilove,
Shreveport, La.,

Dear Sir:

Mr. Jouett and I wish to take adoption papers on Patricia Tarper, the little girl, who was deserted by her parents in December.

We have had the *since* Dec. 28, 1932, the day her parents left her. She has grown into our hearts so much that we do not want to give her up.

I am teaching here and Mr. Jouett is a groceryman at 130 Louisiana St., Shreveport. phone 27887. If there is any question — he will be glad to answer.

Thanking you, I am,

Very truly yours,
Elizabeth Reese Jouett
(Mrs. J. B.)

Left and Found

Dear Mother and Dad,

You just don't know how very much I would love to see you,
And I feel so strongly that you would love to see me too.
So many years ago, you were forced to abandon little Michael and me,
In a courtroom as we slept you slipped away, how hard it had to be.
But times were hard and The Great Depression was sweeping our land,
You had tried every way and there was no place to turn,
I really understand.
A newspaper reporter saw Michael and it touched his heart,
But Michael was very sick, and three days later he died,
Without a second start.
I was adopted by parents & a granny who loved me dearly too.
They cared for me and raised me the best way that they knew.
I found this poem I started many years ago, and once again
I read it through,
My thoughts have not changed, they are still honest and true.
But the verses I add will bring new meaning to me,
A dream, a wish I thought could never come true, has you see.
I've found a sister I never knew I had,
But time and years have taken my mother and dad.
I'm so happy it's hard to express how I feel at this point in time,
To have found a sister who is truly mine.
I want to thank my daughter Doricia for her loving and caring call,
And my son Joey who searched and searched and gave it his all.
And thank you Heavenly Father for letting my dream come true,
These blessings you've given to me no one else could ever do.

Patricia LeRoy
June 13, 1993

I Remember Mama
(A True Story)

I remember Mama in a very special way,
And as the years go by, I miss her more each day.
She was the only mama that I ever knew
Because I was deserted at the age of two.

My little brother Michael and I
Were abandoned by parents desperate with despair,
The depression and no job or money,
They could only love us and care.

In a courtroom full of people,
They slipped out and left us asleep,
With no thought for themselves,
And their hurt was so deep.

But the toll was too much for Michael to bear,
And the 3 days he passed away just seven months old.
Then I was alone but was so blessed to be
Adopted by a mama, daddy and a granny too I was later told.

A neighbor told me one day,
"You are adopted, no one ever wanted you."
But momma said, "Please don't cry.
We love you, that's just not true. "

Mama saved all the newspaper stories about Michael and me,
Because she knew one day all of the clippings I'd want to see.
She had an understanding and knew just what to do or say,
And smiles and hugs and kisses were given every day.

She was only foot eight in height,
But she always stood up for what she believed was right.

I was very spoiled, to be sure,
But I grew up knowing the right things to do.
Sometimes I must have disappointed you in things I said or did,
I'm so sorry. I never meant to hurt you.

She taught me many things
To help and guide me along life's road,
And always told me to trust Jesus,
He will lighten your load.

Then came the time when her health failed,
Her eyesight dimmed and she felt despair,
She was so small and frail, I felt helpless
And now I could only love her and care.

I'll always miss you mama and your very special ways,
And I try to live so you would be proud of me every day.
And to mama I never knew, I wish I could tell you,
I understand and I love you too.

Pat LeRoy
April 1989

Read in Church – Mother's Day 1989

Chapter Three

Back in the Day

I remember falling asleep in Granny's big four-poster bed while she told me my favorite stories. She would sit on the front porch steps and watch me slide down the hill across the street on a piece of cardboard until I was too tired to play anymore. I wore out many of daddy's cardboard boxes from his grocery store. Sometimes Daddy would make me a playhouse with a front door and windows out of a big cardboard box. Granny would take the old Sears catalog and cut pictures of mommies, daddies, babies, and some furniture. We would play all afternoon. Even though she was deaf, she always understood me. My granny was very, very special to me all my life. I loved her dearly. I have to be honest and say she spoiled me good fashion! Mama always said that she was a married "old maid" school teacher. She was strict too. She and daddy owned a little neighborhood grocery store. Daddy was proud of his store because he never had a chance to finish school and had made it on his own. I loved to hear Daddy's stories about when he was a little boy and his family was crossing Texas in a covered wagon. They settled in Plano, Texas. Now, believe me, daddy thought there was no place like Texas. Also, Mama was from Kentucky and she thought there was no place like Kentucky. Therefore, while some folks might fuss over money or other things Mama and Daddy had an ongoing "thing" about which was the best state, Texas or Kentucky!

Mama thought a proper breakfast was oatmeal, eggs, bacon, and toast. Sometimes daddy and I would go to the store early and he would cut a steak from the meat market. Meat did not come pre-packaged in those days. Then he would get a stick of butter and an onion, cook the steak and sliced onions on the grill, and get a loaf of fresh soft Wonder Bread to eat with it. I will never forget how good it was. One day, Mama came in early to work and there we were enjoying that steak! She was very upset and we were back to eating oatmeal, bacon, eggs, and toast. Nevertheless, you have to admit mama was way before her time. She did not realize how healthy oatmeal was for you and that it helped to control cholesterol.

Mama was quite social, she belonged to the Bridge Club and the Kentucky Club and several other organizations. Sometimes she would take me with her and I would end up in the kitchen watching the cooks prepare the refreshments. They always gave me samples and that was fun. Therefore, of course, I always wanted to go with mama to all of her meetings. I loved working at daddy's store, he would let me sweep the floor and dust the shelves of canned goods. One day when I had worked very hard, Daddy gave me a watermelon and I wanted to carve my name on it. I went to the meat counter and picked up a knife to carve my name and it slipped and cut my thumb. It took three stitches to sew up my thumb. It was such a foolish thing for me to do and I never carved my name on anything else again.

We always had a nanny goat even when we lived in town. Daddy believed that goat's milk was healthier than cow's milk. The Goat Dairy gave Daddy little baby triplet goats one time. They were so cute. The Carnation milk representative came to the store and mama told him they had triplet babies; then she laughed and told him they were baby goats. He thought it was so funny that he sent a case of Carnation Milk for the triplets. It was my job to fix the bottles for the baby goats. One morning I went to fix the bottles and the can was not open, so I decided to open the can myself by using an ice pick. The first hole was fine, but when I tried to put the second hole in the top, the ice pick missed the top of the can and went through my finger! Now that was painful. I never picked up another ice pick until I was grown. One day the nanny goat got out of the back yard and chewed up a shirt on the clothesline next door. The woman was so mad, but Daddy replaced the shirt. Goats will eat the paper from tin cans, but they also enjoy chewing on clothes.

Left and Found

A Letter To Daddy

Remember how I followed you like a little shadow
Just about everywhere you went
When you called me snibblefretz I loved it
It was a special name you give me

I played in the grocery store while you checked your books
Sometimes I went with you to buy fresh vegetables at the
market near Red River

One time you took me with you to deliver grocery to jail
I saw men behind the bars and I was very afraid
So I hid behind you and you took my hand to let me know that I
was safe

You often teased me and said, "Patsy I could have retired a millionaire
if you hadn't eaten up all my profit in candy."

You made me little books from the brown grocery paper on a roll
I had so much fun drawing pictures you made me feel so special

Remember one Sunday during church – I rolled the church program
And pretended it was a cigarette
How embarrassing it was for you being a deacon in the church
That was a spanking I well deserved!

You know that you, mama and granny spoiled me good fashion
And I try to live each day in a way you would be proud of me

Then came the time you sold your grocery store and retired
You were getting old your health was beginning to fail
I really didn't want to leave you and go oversees

Just before our tour was over God called you home
I didn't even get to say "goodbye"
That was so very hard for me
And I'm so thankful for all the wonderful memories

As time goes by, I miss you more & more
But I know in my heart I will see you again
I'll say "hello and I love you daddy!"

Patricia LeRoy

At that time, we lived in a big white house on Louisiana Avenue almost in front of Hamilton Terrace Jr. High School. Our back gate opened to the school grounds. It was nice to be so close to school but sometimes, I would still be tardy. I really enjoyed going to school. Those were the days when we all looked forward to recess. I vote to bring back recess again! Spanish was taught as a subject, which was way before its time. One of the reasons recess was so great was because Daddy brought me a special treat every day. I guess you could say that I was very spoiled. The scariest thing that ever happened to me occurred while we lived on Louisiana Avenue. A huge pipe started near our house and ran underground. I could almost stand up in it. It went the full length across the front of Hamilton Terrace Jr. High School. The pipe was near the sidewalk and sometimes we would play in it. This one particular day I was going to daddy's store and for the fun of it, I decided to go through the pipe. About half way through the pipe, I heard a noise. I looked back and there was a man. He yelled at me to stop, but I was so scared I ran faster and began to cry. I was so afraid I would fall or trip before I got to the end of the pipe. When I got to the end of the pipe, I scrambled up to the sidewalk and ran all the way to daddy's store, which was three blocks away. I was so scared. I was crying so hard I could hardly tell Daddy what had happened. He went right away to check the pipe, but the man had fled. I must have had an angel watching over me. I never played in that pipe again.

Not long after that, we moved to the country. It was fun living out in the country. There was a big chinaberry tree in the yard. The grass would not grow under it, so it was perfect for a playhouse. I would sweep it clean and draw lines in the ground for the rooms. Daddy made me chairs, a table, and a bed from apple crates for my doll. I would play for hours in my special playhouse. One afternoon I decided I would climb the tree. To my dismay, I fell and broke my left arm. After that, no more climbing trees for me. Then we moved back into town to 1118 Mildred Street. It was a beautiful big old house with a big living room and dining room; the doors slid into the walls. It had the most beautiful and neatest stairway that had a landing half way up that went upstairs and into the kitchen. I have never seen a stairway like that again. Across the street was a park. It took up a whole block. It had swings, slides, seesaws, and many benches and tables. It even had a tennis court. In the summer, there would be classes in all kinds of crafts. The best classes were the ones where we made belts from "toe" sacks, felt belts, and wooden clogs. We neighborhood kids would play in the park all day and sometimes until dark. Our school was about eight blocks away; we would walk together, and sometimes we would walk home for lunch. This was the 1940's and we saved our dimes to fill a booklet that would buy a $25 war bond. My granny bought several bonds for me. While daddy still owned his store, he and mama were invited to a political rally for Huey P. Long when he was running for Governor of Louisiana. I remember it was the biggest barbecue I had ever been to. I had never seen so many people in one place.

Mama and Daddy were always going somewhere and most of the time they took me with them. Guess that is why I love to travel and go places. Every chance I get I have one foot in the road! One summer Aunt Martha, granny, and I took a trip to see daddy's sister, Aunt Lizzie, who lived in Kemah, Texas. She lived two blocks from the beach on the Gulf of Mexico. Every day I went swimming with two girls who lived next door to Aunt Lizzie. One evening we were swimming and the tide began to go out before we knew it. That was scary. The last Saturday before we left, my friends and I took a ferry to another town to see the movie "Dancing in the Rain" starring Gene Kelly. The ferry ride was very special. I will always remember my trip to see Aunt Lizzie. She was so sweet to us.

After Church on Sunday, Daddy and Mama liked to take a drive in the country. One Sunday, we went to see Aunt Myra and Uncle Harry. They had a big house out in the country. I always loved to visit them. Aunt Myra asked me if I would like to go with her to visit a neighbor. Of course, I said yes. When we got there, she introduced me to her friends and then her friends introduced us to their guest. Her name was Lena Horne. I did not realize she was a movie star and singer until later when Aunt Myra told me. I remember Lena Horne for the song she made famous, "Stormy Weather." At this time, daddy still owned his neighborhood grocery store. Later, due to Mama and Daddy's health they had to sell their store and retire.

Now Daddy could pursue a dream he had for years. Several times, he had driven to Arkansas because he loved the mountains. Each time he looked for a place to buy so he could retire there. Then he found a small farm on Highway 71, south of Hatfield, Arkansas, population 230, and he bought it. The house sat on a slate hill. It was an old house with an open hallway through the middle with the living room and kitchen to one side and the bedrooms on the other side. There was a porch all the way across the front and a side porch beside the kitchen. In addition, there was an "outhouse" out back. There was no electricity or running water. We were really "roughing it" compared to living in the city. Mama cooked on a wood cook stove and the food was delicious. There was just something special about food cooked on a wood cook stove. We had to draw all our water from the well and fill the Aladdin lamps with oil every day. The big heater had to be in the living room, and it had to be kept filled with coal in the wintertime because it really got cold at night. I would sink down in the feather bed with lots of quilts on top; you had better get comfortable because it was almost impossible to move. Mama would put a big galvanized tub near the big heater and heat hot water on the stove. She would fill the tub so we could bathe. These are some of my best memories.

Life was more laid back in the middle 1940's. After all the chores had been done, we had time to sit on the front porch and watch the cars go by and just relax until time to do evening chores. Mama and daddy were enjoying their retirement. Since the farm was small, about twenty acres I think. They had one cow, one horse, one pig, and lots of goats and chickens. Mama loved the animals, especially pig-pig; when she went out to feed them, they all came running. When it came time to butcher pig-pig, mama could not do it so daddy had to buy another pig to butcher. I learned how to milk the goats and the cow, but milking was not as hard as separating the cream was. The milk was called raw milk and the heavy cream would rise to the top. It sure was good on hot oatmeal in the morning. We would drive to Mena on Monday, go to the laundry, and wash clothes on a wringer washer. Now, that was hard work. Then we would go back home and hang all the clothes on the clothesline to dry. The next day we would iron everything; that was it until the next Monday. My clothes would smell like cedar because mama would run the flat iron she heated on the stove over cedar limbs and then iron my dresses. My Granny still lived with us and she was getting old, but she was just as sweet and special as ever. She was still sewing and making some of my dresses. Daddy would buy the feed for the animals in flowered sacks, and he would buy enough sacks alike to make me a dress. When the sacks were washed and ironed, the material was very nice. I remember one special dress granny made me. It had peplum around the waist and it was my favorite.

Have you ever eaten fresh fried chicken? Every Sunday morning mama would get up early, wring a chicken's neck, dress it, and put it in cold salt water until we got home from church. Then she would fry it on the wood cook stove and make milk gravy. You could call it "fittin." Then she would cook great northern beans, collards, and corn meal dumplings; they were "fittin" too.

This was 1945 and I was a ninth grader and going to start high school at Hatfield. It was quite different from the big city school I had gone to in Shreveport. There was only one school building. The elementary school classes were downstairs and the high school classes were upstairs. Mr. Musgrave was the Principal and his wife was the home economics teacher. We learned to cook and sew in a small cottage beside the school. Since Mama was a retired teacher, sometimes she would substitute in the elementary classes. The folks in Hatfield were so friendly and made us feel so welcome. I remember my very first best friend, Helen (Britton) Fortner. We shared many good times together. Then I met Kathleen (Griffin) Gray, Opal Fern (Taylor) Smith, Wanda Jean (Miller) Mc Daniels, Aldena McCaferty, Terrance Powell, Hilton Bell, Calvin Richards, Denver Borders, Johnny Craig, Betty June (Burgess) Slote, Mary Lynn (Ross) Harris, Claudia (Stricklin) Critser, Mary Ella (Foley) Lane, Billie Dale (Johnson) Corella, Bonnie (Stricklin) Richardson, Marquita Lloyd, Warren Fretz, and last but not least, Ivan Gore. All through the years, we have all remained good friends and looked forward to the class reunions. How great it was to see old friends and to reminisce about the "good old days." The last class reunion I was able to go to was our 50th. It was so special and the memories are priceless. All my friends wrote in my journal and we had a group picture taken. We have lost a few dear classmates, but we will never forget them. I did not graduate at Hatfield, because we moved to Mena, the County Seat, when I was in the 11th grade, I graduated from Mena High School. I enjoyed going there, but it just was not the same as Hatfield. My heart belongs to my Hatfield friends and classmates. In addition, it is so nice to be remembered and to be invited to the Hatfield Class reunions. Since we all graduated in 1949, we call ourselves the 49ers; very appropriate, don't you think?

I love the saying "Back in the Day." It sure brings back great memories of days past when we were teenagers in high school. Life was simple but good. Friendships we made would last our lifetime. Our parents were strict but fair. No nonsense was tolerated much less thought about. And I'm sure we were silly at times, but that was to be expected. Many of our classmates have passed away, but we will never forget them. As these thoughts crossed my mind, I began to think about writing a poem. I called it "Another Place in Time." It made me think about how times have changed. In 2014, our class celebrated its 65th class reunion. My goodness, our class reunion is old enough to draw Social Security!

When I lived in Hatfield, life was simple, and it was great! There was only one movie theater and it featured one show a week. The seats were like picnic benches, but we did not care as none of us really watched the movie. We were enjoying just being with our boyfriends. Do you remember those days? About two years later, a new theater was built and it was nice, but we really missed the old theater where we had all the fun. The one time I ever remembered putting one over on daddy was the night Kathleen had a slumber party and we all went to the movies. Daddy was going to pick us up and take us to Kathleen's house from the movies. However, Kathleen's boyfriend, Ted came and they left early. What were we going to do when Kathleen was not with us when daddy came? Well, we had to think fast, so one of the girls pretended to be Kathleen and we all crowded in daddy's van talking to "Kathleen." When we got to her house, we all hurried to get out of the van; I gave Daddy a big kiss. He never knew, and I never told him that Kathleen was not with us.

Ivan was my first boyfriend; I always thought he looked like Victor Mature. His family owned the local phone exchange. We had an old-fashioned wooden phone on the wall. There were five families on each party line. Our ring was two short, one long. You could hear all the others on the party line pick up their phones too. I guess that was the best way to keep up with "all the latest news." At one of our class reunions, his wife Lou Ann told me she wanted to tell me one of the stories Ivan had told her from when we were going together. I said "OK" and she related this story to me. She said, "Patsy, Ivan said he came to see you one evening and walked outside with you to throw out the dishwater and he gave you a kiss. Then Lou Ann said, "Do you remember what you said to Ivan"? I said, "No, what did I say to Ivan?" Lou Ann said, "You said to Ivan, 'you call that a kiss'?" Then Ivan told Lou Ann, "Then I laid one her." Then we both had a good laugh about this. I always like to spend the night with Wanda Jean and ride the old wooden school bus to school. Betty June's mother made the best saccharine sour pickles I ever ate. I cannot forget the delicious chocolate gravy and biscuits Aldena's mother made. Have you ever eaten chocolate gravy? You just do not know what you have missed; it is very easy to make. Here is the recipe:

Chocolate Gravy

1 cup sugar
3 tablespoons all-purpose flour
3 tablespoons cocoa
2 cups milk
2 egg yolks (lightly beaten)
2 teaspoons vanilla extract

Stir together sugar, flour, and cocoa in medium saucepan.
Stir in milk and egg yolks.
Cook over low heat; stir constantly about 25 minutes or until thick.
Add vanilla.
Serve on hot biscuits. Yum! Yum!

I think I could write a book about Hatfield. While we lived at Hatfield, Uncle Harry and Aunt Myra came to visit us. They still lived in Shreveport, Louisiana. Uncle Harry woke up with chest pains early one morning and Daddy took him to Mena to the doctor. The doctor examined him and told him he thought he had indigestion and if it didn't go away to come back and see him. Later that morning Uncle Harry passed away from a heart attack. They had no children and Aunt Myra was devastated about Uncle Harry. After the funeral, she was just lost. One of her prize possessions was her parrot named Polly; Aunt Myra gave Polly to me. Then she went to Bogg Springs near Hatton, Arkansas, where she stayed for several weeks. She just gave up; she would not eat and wrote seven wills. All of it was just too much for her and she passed away. It was so sad. Now Polly was quite the bird! She talked and sang so much you would have to cover her cage to get her to hush. If you did not cover her cage very well, she would peep out and keep right on talking. One time I tried to pet her and she bit my thumb. Believe me, it hurt; her beak was sharp. When Aunt Myra gave me, Polly, daddy was upset and said," I won't have that bird in the house!" Well, wouldn't you know it, Daddy became very fond of Polly. At first, she would sit on his finger then she would sit on his arm and later she would walk up to his arm and sit on daddy's shoulder. I believe he enjoyed Polly more than he ever admitted. Sometimes when Daddy would eat, Polly would sit on his shoulder. Daddy would have a bite of biscuit, sorghum syrup, and butter, and then Polly would have a bite. It was a sight to see. When Polly got old and died, I know daddy missed her so much. In 1948, we moved from Hatfield to Mena, which was the County Seat; daddy had bought a house on Janssen Avenue across from the park. Mena had a beautiful park. I enrolled in Mena High School and completed the eleventh grade and half of the twelfth grade. I then took the other half of my twelfth grade English from the University of Arkansas. I had enough credits to finish in eleven and a half years, and then I graduated in May with my class from Mena High School.

Another Place in Time

Take me to another place in time
Where folks loved and cared
Where rivers and streams were fresh and clear
And the air we breathed was pure
Where music was a guitar on Saturday night
And a cake walk was fun with someone special
When a handshake meant a promise kept
With plenty of time for chores with time left over
Then time took on a faster pace
No more time to sit on the old front porch
And wave to friends and strangers alike
With the sweet aroma of lavender wisteria
And a gentle breeze brushing across your face
No more time for other folks
And no more time to stroll down memory lane
Then it was hurry here and hurry there
Now came the worry and the stress
This old world is in such a rush
So many demands and so little time
Oh, how our life has changed
Please take me back to another place in time

Patricia LeRoy

Chapter Four

A New Journey

After we moved to Mena, I met Ronnie Goss; he was in my English class. He was very nice and soon we were seeing each other. While Ronnie and I were dating, he owned his own jukebox and pinball machine company. He was very good with electronics; he did his own repair work. He was also the projectionist at the local movie theater. He was a young entrepreneur. Miss Kirsch, our English teacher, teased me about getting a book I would enjoy because she knew I was doing Ronnie's book reports. Ronnie and I became very serious and by graduation, we were planning to get married. We were married in June 1949 at the Methodist Church. We were young and in love; no one could tell us anything. We had a cute little house and were very happy. Mickie was our firstborn, and then Beth was born while her father was stationed in Korea with the Arkansas National Guard. It was wonderful when he came home, and soon we moved to Little Rock, Arkansas. Ronnie enrolled in a school for radio and TV. Soon he had a job at KARK-TV and he was really enjoying it. Well, by then, I was expecting again and Joey was born. We bought a house, but things were just not the same. We realized we had married too young and decided the best thing to do was to get a divorce.

You know we all have cute stories about our children. I would like to share a few with you. When Mickie was learning to put on his shoes and socks, he asked me which was the right sock and which was the left sock. The story about the socks was cute, but Mickie was smart. In Junior High School, he did a math paper about the population explosion. His teacher said it was worthy of a college grade. I was very proud of him. He called Beth "BeBe;" and we still call her BeBe. When BeBe was just a few weeks old, she woke me up crying. I ran to her baby bed. I could see by her night light something black and fuzzy. I thought it was a spider and I noticed her leg was red and swollen. I called my doctor and he told me to bring BeBe and put the fuzzy black spider in an envelope and come to the emergency room. I got BeBe and the envelope and rushed to the hospital. My doctor was waiting for us. He took BeBe and the envelope into the emergency room. Soon I heard laughing. What could be so funny? My doctor came out with BeBe and he was still laughing. He told me her leg was swollen from her DPT shot, and the spider was a piece of black yarn. Then I remember mama had recovered my comforter and had tied it with black yarn. I was so relieved that I had to laugh too. For a long time, my doctor teased me about the black yarn spider. When Joey was about four years old, we were at grandpa's farm in Kentucky. Joey found a little worm in the garden; he put it in his hand and went to show grandpa. When he went to show him the worm, it began to move around. Joey said, "Be still worm." The worm was still moving so Joey said again, "Be still worm." Then he came down with his hand and the worm went splat! Now the little worm was forever still. Joey loved mama's cooking and would say, "Mama this tastes like good."

The children and I stayed in Little Rock; one day I saw in the newspaper that the American Red Cross was offering a First Aid Class. It sounded like a class I would enjoy, as I had at one time wanted to be a nurse. I took a real interest in first aid and took all the classes offered, and the instructor's class. Since I was the smallest person in our class, I was usually the victim. Therefore, I was rescued from all sorts of situations like up and down stairs and pulled out of car windows and house windows. When I received my Instructor's Card, I laughed and said, "I am not sure what kind of instructor I will be, but if you need a victim let me know." Teaching first aid was very special to me and I never missed an opportunity to teach. I got to work at the State Fair Red Cross tent and the flood disaster. I will never forget these experiences. Through the years, I received many awards, certificates, and letters of appreciation, but my most special award is my Humanitarian Medal from the National Red Cross in Washington, D.C. I volunteered for the Red Cross for over 33 years. You know, you have not done anything for anyone unless it is from your heart, and that is a great feeling. When I retired from teaching First Aid, I had taught 4,500 hours.

Chapter Five

Service Life

My neighbor told me about a great job as a receptionist for a doctor; his name was Dr. Howard B. Strauss, III. He was very nice to work with, and I really enjoyed my job. While working for Dr. Strauss, I met a Staff Sergeant named Philip LeRoy. He was stationed at Little Rock Air Force Base (AFB). He was somewhat quiet and I liked him right away. We began to date and three months later, we drove to Mississippi and were married. It was November 1957. Two years later, Kevin was born. When he was 3 months old, Phil got orders to go to Barksdale Air Force Base in Shreveport, Louisiana, for training. We lived in a Motel for 4 weeks, and then Phil received Permanent Change of Station (PCS) orders for Seymour Johnson Air Force Base in Goldsboro, North Carolina, for a new squadron called MMS (Munitions Maintenance Squadron). Phil's commanding officer was Major Manley and the children called the MMS squadron their own special name, Major Manley's Squadron. One time in the 1960's, the Base paid all the military in $2.00 bills. They wanted the people to know how much money the Base personnel spent here. I have never seen so many $2.00 bills! When we arrived in Goldsboro, there was not a single house to rent, so we had to live in a motel. That is not easy with four children. Therefore, we decided to buy a house. What else could we do? However, it turned out to be the best decision we made. Several months after we became homeowners, along came Lucinda. We lived about two miles from the Base. I enjoyed service life, although it was quite different from the life I had always known. After Lucinda, along came Shannon. Because he was born on mama's birthday, she said he was the nicest birthday present she ever got. In 1964, Phil received PCS orders for Okinawa. This would be a real life changing experience for me. I have to admit it sounded exciting. We put an ad in the paper to rent our home. A lady called about renting and the first words out of her mouth were," I just want you to know we are not military." Then Phil said, "We are military and our home is not for rent to you." Well, it was just another case against the military. You know we are just ordinary folks just as you except we have chosen the military life, which is quite different from civilian life. You need to remember that our husbands are always on call, always ready to go to wherever needed to defend our country, and for freedom for everyone! We rented our house and the children and I moved to Mena to be near my mama and daddy until we went overseas to join Phil. It was wonderful to be near mama and daddy and visit with them every day. The children sure enjoyed being spoiled by grandpa and grandma.

Before we went overseas, we went to visit Phil's mom and dad. I cannot leave out a little story about Lucinda (Cindy). We were coming back from a visit to Phil's dad's farm in Kentucky and Lucinda said," Mama I got to go." I said, "Honey there is no place to go along this highway." She said, "Mama I really got to go." Phil pulled over to the side of the road. She jumped out, pulled down her little panties, sat down on the ground, and spread her dress out all around her. Then she got up, pulled her panties up and straightened out her dress, got in the car as if it was nothing. You have heard of "Twinkle, Twinkle Little Star?" Well, I refer to that as "Tinkle, Tinkle Little Cindy." Looking back now, the time went by so fast and before too long Phil had orders for us to join him in Okinawa. Mama and daddy were so old and it was so hard to say good-by.

Soon we were on our way to California and then on to Okinawa on a Military Air Transport Service plane. We made our first stop in Alaska. This was 1964 right after the earthquake and I remember looking out the window of the plane at the devastation from the earthquake. I had never seen anything like that before. It looked like everything was destroyed or damaged. Our stop was a brief one and we were on our way again. Our next stop was in Japan where our American flight attendants got off and our Asian flight attendants got on the plane. Then it seemed only a short time in the air before they announced we would be landing in Okinawa. It was about midnight and as I looked down at Okinawa, it looked like a huge lit up Christmas tree. As we reached the bottom of the steps from the plane, Phil was waiting for us. We sure were happy to see him. He had rented us a little house right outside Naha Air Force Base. There were lots of houses and soon we met our neighbors who were all military too. The next morning I realized how different Okinawa was from home. The people were different but very friendly. The trees and flowers were also different, very beautiful, and so colorful. Of course, the food did not look or taste like the food at home. I soon learned to appreciate how healthy and tasty it was. We lived at Naha for several months until Phil changed from being in a Strategic Air Command to a Tactical Air Command. He was transferred to Kadena AFB. We had to wait for base housing and lived off base in Kadena Circle; we lived there until Phil could get into base housing. It was quite an experience to live on the economy. Not far from Kadena Circle was a one-cent store that was right, everything was one cent! The Japanese candy was unique because the outside wrapper was made from rice paper and could be eaten. Everything in the store was specially wrapped or came with a small toy. The candy suckers were so neat. There were several flavors and when the wooden stick was dipped in liquid flavored candy, twisted and held up, the candy sucker was completely hard and ready to enjoy. All the children loved the one-cent store. What was there not to love?

We really enjoyed living in Kadena Circle because we really got a chance to meet and know the Okinawan people. We could see how polite they were. It did not take long to see that the people were not as different as I first thought. Sometimes several of us wives would get together and go shopping. Now, that was a super experience! In Naha, there was a special place to shop called "Black Market Alley." What a place, just one little shop after another. It was located at the Oki-Dinki (the big red light) and the favorite place to shop to find just about anything from dishes, glassware, quilts, every sewing need, crafts, scarves, etc. There was the thirty-cent store. What a place, the thirty-cent store! Yes, everything was only thirty cents. Most of the people spoke some English. Thank goodness, they used American currency. Oh, my! Their toy stores were every child's fantasy. There were beautiful dolls, China dishes, fantastic robots, and airplanes with lights and real sounds; the doors opened and closed. Many of these toys required batteries, but they were so unique we had to have them. There were all kinds of marbles and even Christmas lights. The shelves were jam packed with games; there were many unique wooden banks. Also, a big department store was as fancy and modern as any department store stateside. Koza City, outside of Gate 2 at Kadena AFB, was great shopping.

Several months later, we moved into base housing on Kadena AFB. Doricia was born at Camp Kue Military Hospital. While I was expecting Doricia, I developed a serious blood clot in my left thigh. I was in Camp Kue for 10 days. The next month, I had Doricia and developed another blood clot. I did not get to hold my baby for six days. A nurse felt sorry for me, put me in a wheelchair, and took me to the nursery to see my baby. The doctor told my husband I would not live to leave the hospital. I was devastated! I prayed and asked God to please let me live long enough to see my children grown. God granted me more than that. I have seen my seven children grown, grandchildren, and even great-grandchildren. What a wonderful, loving, caring, Heavenly Father we have.

By this time, Kevin and Cindy were in school and Shannon was 4 years old. He wanted to go to school too. I went to the youth center and talked to the director about Shannon going to 4-year-old kindergarten. It was expensive and I asked if they were going to serve cookies for snacks. The director said yes and I asked him if I could bake them and how many he would need. He figured it out and called to tell me he would need 120 dozen cookies. I said that would be fine and I sent Shannon to kindergarten. What a deal! I have always loved to cook and bake, so it was not a hard task for me. Do you know anyone who sent their child to pre-kindergarten for 120 dozen cookies? Most likely not! I have to tell you this story about Shannon: The first week I drove Shannon and my friend's son to school. The next week it was her turn to drive the children to school. We were sitting on the steps waiting for her. When she drove up, I kissed Shannon and told him to go get in her car. He looked at me and said," No!" Again, I told him to get in the car. He looked at me and said, "I am not going to get in that Volkswagen; call me a taxi." I could not believe what he said, even though it was funny. I just could not get him to get in her car. Finally, I told her to go on; I took Shannon in the house and I am not sure what strategy I used, but the next morning he was waiting on the steps for her.

The Noncommissioned Officers' Club had family night once a week. It was great to eat out and see a floorshow as well. One night the special performer was country singer Little Jimmie Dickens. His show was very good, and he signed my table card for me. I thought that was special. I was not sure I would enjoy my overseas tour, but I loved it.

The Okinawa culture was so interesting and the climate was ideal, except for typhoon season. The Island was surrounded by water, the China Sea on one side and the Pacific Ocean on the other side. It was the bluest water I have ever seen. There were so many things to see, places to visit. There was suicide cliff, where many Japanese soldiers jumped off the cliff and killed themselves. Many beautiful monuments commemorated the history of suicide cliff. There was a cave of the virgins, where it is said 150 high school girl students and their teachers committed suicide to keep from surrendering to the American soldiers. The cave was sealed, but visitors could buy flowers to put at the front of the cave in their memory. The Glass Factory, where they did beautiful glass blowing, was another interesting place to visit. They made pitchers, glasses, bowls, and fruits, which were hand made from old glass, like soda pop bottles, or any glass bottles or jars. The colors were so vibrant and beautiful. The factory where they made dolls was also an experience; just to see all the handwork and detail on each doll showed how dedicated they were. Then there was a sugar cane factory and the flour factory, the snake and turtle factory where they made belts and other accessories. It made me sad over what happened to the turtles to make these items. One of the biggest crops was the pineapple fields; the pineapples were delicious and very cheap. One of the most memorable places I visited was the beautiful garden where a peace statue was being constructed; the man constructing this was in his 80's. The Buddha was huge and sat on a Lotus flower with his hands outstretched in love. The composition of the statue was composed of dirt, sand, and precious and semiprecious stones from all over the world. He wanted his statue to represent Peace for the World. The Buddha was so huge they had to build the building around the statue.

Martial arts were very popular in Okinawa. The most famous cultural sport of Okinawa was karate, which is thought to be part Chinese Kung Fu and part Okinawa martial arts. Karate demands respect and seriousness and is regarded in high esteem. Kevin, Cindy, Shannon, and I all took karate classes and earned our Brown Belts. There are many styles of karate; the style we learned is Shorinryu Matsumura Orthodox Karate and Kubudo. We also learned Kodokan Judo. Our karate club traveled all over Okinawa doing demonstrations and tournaments. While we were in Okinawa, our children competed in many tournaments and won lots of awards and certificates. Kevin, Cindy, and Shannon also took Judo and earned their Brown Belts. In learning Judo and karate, many lessons were learned including self-discipline. I always told them that when you go to a tournament do your best to win, that is all that is required, but if you lose, be a good sport. Never go in with the attitude that if you win OK, if you lose, OK, that is not acceptable.

One Judo tournament was exciting. Shannon was competing against a boy from the Army Judo Club. The other boy was bigger than Shannon and when it seemed he was about to lose his team-mates began to yell, "Shannon do what you did at class!" Well, he did and threw the boy off the mat with a sweeping technique and won. Cindy also competed and the referee tied a red ribbon around her waist to tell the girls apart. Cindy threw the other girl and when they returned to their places, the referee thought the other girl won. Even though it was not fair, you did not question or correct the Okinawa referee. I told Cindy we knew the other girl did not win fair and she knew this too. Now it was Kevin's turn to compete. The other boy got Kevin on the mat in a chokehold and he was turn-ing blue. Well, I completely forgot that you do not ever correct the Okinawa referee and I jumped from the front row of the bleachers. I ran to the mat and said to the referee, "Are you going to let him choke Kevin?" He looked at me and then told the other boy to let him up. When Kevin got up, he went into a karate stance! I was yell-ing, "Kevin, Kevin, this is not karate this is Judo!" He told me later that above all the screaming, yelling, and noise from the crowd, he heard his mama yelling at him. I guess you could say this was just another exciting day of our tour in Okinawa. Kevin told me later he had gone into defense mode as he had fought that boy before and won. The other boy wanted to hurt Shannon because he had lost to him in other Judo tournaments.

Now here is the "twist" to this story. Before we left to come home, Kevin's instructor wanted him to go for the third-degree brown belt, which was unheard of for a seventh grader. When he went for the test, the Okinawa referee was the same one I had gotten upset with at the Judo tournament. I thought he would never pass

Kevin for the test. At this point, his instructor told him that no matter what the referee did or said, "Show no anger." Kevin bowed to show respect to the referee. Then the referee pushed him down, Kevin got up and bowed again; the referee pushed him down again; the referee pushed him down about ten times and each time Kevin showed him respect. Then he put him through the hardest test I have ever seen. However, Kevin made the referee see he was very respectful and knew Judo. Yes, he passed the test. Kevin is my serious child and always has been.

We came home in 1967 and Phil was stationed in Wichita, Kansas, at McConnell Air Force Base. While there, we lived off base housing. Then Phil received orders for Thailand and the children and I went home to Goldsboro. When you are married to a service man, you learn how to take charge when your husband goes overseas. It is a big part of being married to a service man. Then Phil called and said, "We are going back to Okinawa for a second tour." The year was 1969 and once again, we were going overseas. When we got to Okinawa, we lived in Hotel Miami, Koza City; we stayed there for about two months. Every morning the mamasan would fix fried rice with scrambled eggs and soy sauce; our kids loved to eat with them. The people were so nice to us. One night after closing, the owners, Mamasan and Papasan, took us to a beautiful Okinawa restaurant, for the most wonderful supper and entertainment by beautiful Okinawa ladies dressed in their traditional clothes and makeup. They played instruments, sang, and danced for us. It was a night to remember. After we got a house off base, we invited them for dinner. We had turkey and all the trimmings; their favorite was the sweet potatoes with marshmallows. I gave her all the leftovers to take home. Whenever we were in Koza City, we stopped in to see them.

They were always very nice to us and made us feel so welcome. On the first floor of the hotel was a bathhouse and massage, like a spa. One day I decided to try it. They sit you on a stool and use a rough washcloth to scrub you gently and then they pour clean water on you to rinse the soap off. After you are scrubbed clean, you are allowed to step into the tub of hot water; when you get out you are wrapped in a big towel and you lay on a low table while the masseuse massages muscles and even walks on your back. Wow, it felt great! All those special services were only $2.00. Both tours to Okinawa were great memories for all of us. I had a sew girl, Miyoko, who sewed for me both times we were there. Can you believe she only charged $2.00 a day? We would go to the material store and buy beautiful material and she would make dresses for Cindy, Doricia, and me or anything I would ask her to sew. I wanted to bring her home with me, but there was just so much red tape involved. I will always remember her, and all the beautiful things she sewed for us. You could also get a house cleaner for $2.00 a day. Let me tell you, you could easily be spoiled in Okinawa. My sew girl Miyoko taught me how to make delicious dishes. I would like to share these recipes with you.

Okinawan Fried Rice And Yaki Soba*

The secret to delicious fried rice and yaki soba is to prepare all meat and vegetables before you start to cook.

Meat - beef, pork, shrimp, chicken, or ham (cut meat in bite size pieces)

Vegetables - carrots, onions, celery, and bell pepper (cut all veggies on the slant)

Rice - regular rice (<u>Do Not Use Instant Rice</u>) (cook and have ready to add to fried rice)

Sesame Seed Oil, Vegetable Oil, and Soy Sauce

Use Wok or Skillet

Add 3 Tablespoons of vegetable oil and a dash of sesame seed oil (oil and sesame seed oil depend on the amount of meat and vegetables that you are using). Cook meat until done. Add a small amount of soy sauce and mix well. Cook the same with each vegetable. Add rice and mix well. You can use more soy sauce to flavor. If you are using small amounts of meat and vegetables, stir fry meat first, and then add veggies and rice. Be sure to flavor with soy sauce. If you are using a large amount of meat and veggies, cook the meat first and set aside; then cook each veggie and set aside. Then mix together with the rice (add a little soy sauce to the rice to flavor it before adding to meat and veggies) ENJOY! It's so good!

*To make Yaki Soba, use soba noodles instead of rice and the recipe is the same as the fried rice.

Oriental Beef Roast

Real nice beef roast - put in wok or skillet and cover with water. Go around the wok or skillet with soy sauce a few times (not too much) and a dash of sesame seed oil. As the roast cooks, add more water and a little more soy sauce (<u>check roast often to be sure there is enough water</u>). Each time you check the roast, turn the roast over. Test the roast; and when it is done, be sure there is still juice in the bottom of the wok or skillet. Add a little butter to make a sauce for the roast. It is so easy and delicious! Serve with rice.

I set up First Aid Classes and also taught classes no matter where we lived. I got a call from the American Red Cross office in Kadena AFB and was offered the opportunity to be first aid chairperson for the base. Of course, I accepted; it was a chance to do what I really enjoyed. I set up and taught classes. To issue a first aid card, I felt my responsibility was to be sure they were qualified to save a life. My tests were hard and I required a written correct answer. There would be no "true or false" answers or ABCD, or all of the above either. During my training, I used the lecture method of teaching with hands on for artificial respiration, CPR, bandages, and splints.

This is a story about Doricia I want to share with you. We went to the commissary and I bought a bag of candy. Doricia, being the baby, wanted to hold it. She took the bag and she told Kevin, "Here is one piece for you. Shannon here is one piece for you; Cindy here is one piece for you." When they asked for more Doricia said, "No, I am saving this candy for my family in America." Well to be sure, the family in America never got to see that candy.

Chapter Six

Home Again

We came home from our second tour in Okinawa in 1972. We stopped in Shreveport, Louisiana, to see Sue Bell, my adoptive father's daughter. Sue Bell had always been a sweet sister to me. Her sons Thay (and his wife Dana) and Kerlin have always been sweet to me too. I love them all very much. We had such a nice visit together as it had been a long time since I had seen her. We have always kept in touch. While in Shreveport, we went to Juvenile Hall. I asked to see Michael and my folder. I wanted to see if there was any new information that would help me find my birth parents. The woman went to the basement and after awhile came back with an old manila folder. She looked inside at the papers and told me there was a letter from my mother. She would not let me see it, nor did she tell me what was in it. Then she said, "Honey, don't try to find them; leave well enough alone." I looked at her and thanked her for finding the folder. I knew in my heart I did not intend to forget about it, but I was not sure what to do next. Then we went to the cemetery where daddy, mama, and granny are buried. As I looked down at their names, it was hard to realize they were gone. It was so sad. We were in Okinawa when my daddy died, and I never had a chance to say good-bye. All of this made me more determined to find my birth parents. Then we drove to Mena, Arkansas, to visit with my mother and my daughter BeBe and her family. While we were there, we went to a nice restaurant. We were sitting at a big round table and this very handsome and charming man was speaking to everyone and shaking his or her hands. He came to our table, shook hands with everyone at our table, and gave me one of his cards. It said, "Bill Clinton." He was running for the office of Governor of Arkansas. I had shaken the hands of a man who would one day be the president of the United States. I had never shaken the hand of a governor or a president before. Bill Clinton was truly charismatic; it was easy to see how he won the vote to become governor of Arkansas and then President of the United States.

Phil's PCS orders from Okinawa took us home again to Seymour Johnson AFB, Goldsboro, North Carolina. It was good to be home again and soon life settled down to normal. The children were all in school and growing up so fast. Then in 1973, Phil received TDY orders for Thailand. Here I was again "in charge" while my husband was overseas. Since all the children were in school, I decided to get a job. I heard about a job as a teacher assistant that sounded like it was perfect for me because I love teaching, especially children. I went to Central Office and put in an application to be a teacher's assistant. A couple days later Mr. Bill Charlton, principal of School Street School, called me and asked me to come in for an interview. I had known Mr. Charlton for a long time. My daughter went to school at School Street School and I had taught karate in a special school program that had also offered other classes like sewing, cooking, and dance. These were fifth graders; the boys really excelled in the karate class, and I was very proud of them and tried to teach them the honor of learning the martial arts. The interview went very well and he hired me. I said to him, "Mr. Charlton, I'll wear long dresses every day." He said, "Every day, Mrs. LeRoy?" I answered, "Yes Sir." He just smiled and told me that was fine. I guess I was before my time wearing long dresses, which are very popular now. Mr. Charlton liked to say "Well" and he said it often. When I retired, he came to speak and said, "I came by to say a few <u>wells</u>!" When we first went to Okinawa, I loved the long dresses and have been wearing them since1964. Today, long dresses are all the rage. I was very excited and could hardly wait for school to start. I soon learned there were many workshops and meetings before school started.

My first job as a teacher assistant was in a fifth-grade class taught by M.B. Brown. We worked very well together. The Government program I was hired for was the Emergency School Aid Act. After 4 years, it was no longer a working program. It sure was a disappointment, as I really loved my job. All summer I kept checking about a job at the school. Then I got a call from Mr. Harvey Davis, Principal of East End School. He asked me to come for an interview as a teacher assistant in a special education class. I told him I had an appointment at 1 O'clock at the base commissary, he said to come by at 12:00. I said I would and after the interview, Mr. Davis said the job was mine if I wanted it. I accepted the job. I was delighted to be teaching children again. I never went to the interview for the base commissary job. I have never regretted this decision. The special education class was quite different from the 5th-grade class. The students were truly special and I fell in love with them. My teacher, Mrs. Janie Williamson, was a very nice person and a great teacher. I learned so much from her; we worked well together for 12 years. We never knew what our special students would say. One day Mrs. Williamson asked Allen, "What sound do you hear when I say frog? Listen good Allen, what sound do you hear when I say frog?" Allen's face lit up and he said, "Ribbitt, ribbitt." Bless his heart; although it was not the answer we hoped for, his answer was perfect.

Later, I was assigned to a Special Education class at Carver Heights School made up of younger students. Again, I was blessed to have a great teacher, Ms. Donna Warren; we worked together for 6 years until I retired. I was 42 years old when I started working; 18 years of this was in Special Education. I retired at age 64. I have such wonderful memories of the years I worked with very special students. I will remember with great love the wonderful teachers with whom I worked. My principal at Carver Heights School was I. K. Williamson. He was a very nice man. He crossed every "T" and dotted every "I," and that was okay with me. When he was transferred to Dillard Middle School, he took our special education class with him. I was so blessed that all of my teachers and principals were Christians and appreciated my devotion to my job. I could write a book about the years I worked in Special Education.

Chapter Seven

Good News at Last

While I was at Carver Heights School, my youngest daughter Doricia decided to make a call to Juvenile Hall in Shreveport, Louisiana, to ask about the sealed records the woman would not let me see so many years before. The women at Juvenile Hall suggested Doricia call the Juvenile Judge and speak to his secretary. Not to be discouraged, Doricia then called Juvenile Court and spoke to the judge's secretary who was nice but firm. Doricia told her my story and that I was 62 years old. She told her I did not want to cause any problems, I just wanted to find my birth parents and tell them I understood about the depression, and how it was they had to leave Michael and me. I needed to tell them I loved them. The secretary then spoke to the judge and he told her to tell Doricia that she and I, needed to write a letter to the judge and send all papers and information I had and he would make a decision about my sealed records.

When Doricia called to tell me this, I could not believe it! I was to say the least beside myself with excitement. I started right away getting everything I had together to send to the judge. I made copies of my birth certificate and adoption papers. I also made copies of all the newspaper stories about Michael and me. I have the original newspaper articles and pictures from 1932-33 from the Shreveport

Times Newspaper. Doricia and I wrote letters to the judge. I registered my package of information and could hardly contain my thoughts and hopes; I also said a prayer of thanks. I just could not believe this was happening after all these years. I had just about exhausted all avenues in my search for my birth parents. I contacted Oprah Winfrey twice, once in 1987 and again 1993. Both times, I received a very nice answer. I had hoped to be on her program and perhaps find my parents that way.

I also wrote to Unsolved Mysteries in 1990 with the hope again that they would tell my story on TV. A woman called me and said it had been too long ago. As it turned out at this time, my birth mother was still living and faithfully watched the program. Who knows why? Maybe perhaps she was hoping to see our story. Then I heard about Four-Point Entertainment in California through a local radio station. I wrote to them in May 1990, but I never heard from them, After Doricia had called the Judge in Shreveport Juvenile Court, I was hearing good news at last.

March 1st 1993

Dear Judge,

    I have enclosed this letter with the things my mother has sent you. To say, I hope you find it in your heart to read the papers + newspaper clippings that she has been holding on for years hoping one day she might write or talk to someone that could help her find the mother and father she has missed for so long. Understanding why they did what they did. They did it for the children not thinking of themselves but only to get care for my mother and Michael. Why would they have travelled so far if not in the interest to find work and to help the family. What I am trying to say is please open your heart and think this could be me. I think to myself all the time "I don't know what I would do without my mom + dad." My mom didn't have a choice nor did her mom + dad but to do what was best for their children. Thank you for the kindness + time of listening to what I have to say concerning my mother,

                Sincerely,
                Doricia

Goldsboro, N.C. 27534
March 1, 1993

Dear Judge,

I am writing this letter in hopes that you will be able to help me. I am enclosing copies of the newspaper stories that my adopted mama saved for me. About 22 yrs ago I went to Juvenile Hall and asked the lady about my file. She went to the basement and got an old folder – it had Michael's and my name on it. There was a letter from my mother asking about Michael and me. I would love to have seen the letter. But I will settle for a copy of the letter and copies of everything in our folder. Michael died and was buried in Green wood Cemetary, now called City Cemetary. I have tried and tried to find his little grave. I want to put a head stone for Michael. No one can seem to tell me anything. I am enclosing a copy of a poem I wrote about mama – and a story I wrote about my life many years ago. I'm so encouraged since my daughter spoke with your secretary. I will appreciate any help Judge. I'm looking forward to hearing from you.

Sincerely,
Patricia

I understood why my birth parents left us; I knew about the Great Depression of the 1930's—a period of crisis in our American history. By 1932, millions of people were unemployed. About a million people wandered from place to place, all over our country in a hopeless search for work, to survive in the hard and so desperate of times. People were begging for just a dime to buy something to eat. It was a struggle just to live from day to day. Families were in dire difficulties just to exist from one day to another. I feel my parents were one of the displaced families of the depression. Some people had to live in old rusted out cars and shacks built of any kind of wood they could find. Sometimes even a big cardboard box was a home for a person or family. Moreover, to be sure, the soup lines were very long for all the hungry people that the depression had caused. These times were the hardest Americans had ever had to face. I pray we will never have another depression like that.

Time seemed endless as I waited daily for the judge's answer. Almost 30 days had passed and I could not stand the wait any longer. I called the judge's office and his secretary told me that the judge had unsealed my records. After 60 years, they were sending copies of the papers in my records. I said, "Thank you so very much. I appreciate everything you all have done to help me." Time seemed even longer as I waited for the package from the judge. I watched every day for the long-awaited papers. At last, it arrived; I opened the package as fast as I could so I could read all the papers. I noticed on one of the papers, a child's name. It said Gertrude Evelyn, born November 1933. Then it hit me, I had a sister! Well, I was overwhelmed and very happy. I was not just searching for my birth mother and father, but for a sister I did not know I had. Some of the papers the judge sent included a nice letter from him; a copy of a letter from mama; which said she and daddy wished to adopt me; and a Juvenile case record of Michael and me being abandoned by desperate parents. It also included a letter from Louisiana State University in Shreveport about Michael dying January 1, 1933, and that he was buried in Greenwood Cemetery; a letter written to Mrs. Sanders, Clint Sander's mother about Michael's death; and a poem written for the Harper children called "Two Little Babes" in The Plain Dealer. Later I obtained a copy of Michael's death certificate. I also have copies of the letters Doricia and I wrote to the judge, along with some more papers I kept. After I had received the package of Court papers, I read them over and over. I remember thinking that with all of this information I would at last be able to find my mother, father, and sister.

About this time, my son Joey called to talk to me. I was so excited I could hardly talk to him. Joey lived in Decatur, Illinois. He said, "Mama, send me copies of the papers and I will help you find them." That was exactly what I did. As soon as Joey received the copies of the papers, he began searching. First, he started with the Veteran's Administration to locate my father. Men are easier to find than women are because men's names do not change. After many phone calls and a lot of talking, Joey learned that my father had passed away at Saint Elizabeth Hospital in 1971. He was unable to find my mother or Gertrude. He called the Social Security office and they told him to tell me to write a letter to my mother and a letter to my sister and take them unsealed to the local Social Security Office. I wrote the letters telling them from my heart how I felt. Then I took them to the Social Security Office. Several weeks later, I received both letters back. I felt like this was my last hope to find them and now it was gone. However, Joey, my detective, was not going to give up that easy. He called the main Social Security office in Baltimore, Maryland, and spoke with a nice woman. He told her he knew about the Freedom of Information Act and asked if she could give him any information about my mother and my sister. She explained that she could not give out that kind of information. Joey told her both the letter to my mother and sister had been returned by the Social Security office in Baltimore. He gave her all the information he had. She said she would run the information through her computer and call him back. Two days later, she called him and said she had some good news and bad news. The good news was she found Gertrude and all the information about her, but she could not give out that information because Gertrude was still living. The bad news was that there was no information on my mother. She told Joey that Gertrude's husband had passed away and she could give him information about him. She told Joey his name and where he was buried. Joey thanked her for her help and started calling all the towns near where Gertrude's husband was buried in Washington State. Within a few minutes, he had the phone number and was talking to my sister. Gertrude told Joey that a day or two before he called she had just received a card from Social Security with my name and phone number on it and was trying to contact me. She said she knew it had to be me, and that she had known about me all her life. Joey asked if she would like to talk to me. Gertrude said yes she would.

Left and Found

Chapter Eight

It's Your Sister

My family, friends, and co-workers at Carver Heights School knew about my search for my mother and sister. I was a teacher's assistant and had worked for Wayne County School for 22 years. When I found Gertrude it was 2 years until I would retire; I retired in 1995.

About 10 o'clock, Joey called Carver Heights School and told the secretary it was an emergency call for me. He also asked to speak to the principal, Mrs. Veda McNair. He explained to Mrs. McNair how he had located my sister and that she would like to speak to me if it would be all right. Mrs. McNair said, "Of course it would be all right," She called our room on the intercom and said, "Pat, you have a call; could you please come to the office?" When I got to the office, it was noisy and she said, "Pat, take your call in my office; it is quieter in there." When I answered the phone, Joey said, "Mama?" I said, ""What's wrong Joey?" Then he said, "Nothing is wrong mama; I have someone on the other line who would like to speak to you." I said," Who is it, sugar?" Joey answered, "It's your sister Gertrude." I remember gasping and my heart began to pound. I was trying to get my thoughts and myself together. Joey had three-way calling and before I knew it, I was crying and talking to Gertrude. What a conversation! She was crying too. My first question was about our mother. How was she? Where was she? Then Gertrude told me she had passed away in 1990. That was not what I wanted to hear; it broke my heart not to get to see her. I had been searching for my mother for so many years to tell her I loved her and that I understood. Now, I would not be able to tell her. Gertrude and I were still crying and talking. Later Joey said," Mama I couldn't get a word in edgewise."

My principal was wonderful and stayed right with me, just as she told Joey she would. After I said good-by, I hung up the phone. I was still so excited and still crying. It is strange how we cry when we are sad, and we cry when we are happy. Was I happy? Yes! Yes! Yes! All my friends were so happy for me too. It did not take long for the "good news" to get around the school. Then I called home to tell my husband Phil that I had talked to Gertrude. He could hardly believe it. I think that maybe he thought that it could not be done. Then I called my children to tell them the wonderful news. They were all very happy for their mama because they all knew how long I had been searching. When I got home from work, I called Gertrude back; we talked and talked. It was a calmer conversation than our conversation at school. We just had so many questions and so much to talk about. It was wonderful. After Gertrude had talked to me at school, she talked to her nephew and left a message on his answering machine. He said later that he was hesitant to return her call because he thought it might be bad news. He thought that maybe something had happened to Uncle Ralph. Uncle Ralph is our mother's only living brother and was in his 80's. However, he did return her call and could not believe that Gertrude and I had found each other after all these years. Then Gertrude's nephew called me. He was so nice on the phone. He also told me he visited my mother many times. My mother had given him a necklace to "give to Patsy if you find her."

Left and Found

He did not know how to find me, but he promised her he would give me the beautiful stone necklace.

In a few days, a package came for me; he had sent me the beautiful necklace. I just cried as I held it in my hand. How very thoughtful of Gertrude's nephew. We talked several times after that. Gertrude and I talked several more times too. Everything was great! I told Gertrude I would love to come see her. We talked about my coming to visit; I planned to go in June when school was out for the summer. I said Gertrude, "Where is Everett, Washington?" She said, "Thirty miles from Seattle." I said, "OK." Then Gertrude said, "Pat, where is Goldsboro, North Carolina." I said, "Fifty miles from Raleigh North Carolina." She said, "OK." We spoke some more about me coming for a visit and meeting her family. She promised me her nephew would be there to meet when I got off the plane in Seattle. Next time we spoke, we laughed about the fact neither of us knew where the other lived and had to get a map to see exactly where Everett and Goldsboro were. My goodness, we were a whole United States apart from east to west.

June 20, 1993

(130 Pages — 9 Sections)

P.O. Box 10629 — Goldsboro, N.C. 27532

Vol. 107—No. 64

Goldsboro
News-Argus

Decades-long search ends in phone call

'It's your sister!'

By LYNN WOOTEN
News-Argus Staff Writer

It was, Patricia LeRoy says, a phone call she had given up hope of ever receiving.

But on June 3 as she was working at Carver Heights Elementary School, Mrs. LeRoy was asked to step to the principal's office.

She had gotten the call, the kind that marks a milestone in someone's personal history — such as a marriage or the birth of a child.

"Hello?" she said.

The caller, her son, Joey, of Decatur, Ill., was barely able to contain his excitement. He explained that he had engaged his three-way, long-distance calling feature and that a third party from Seattle also was on the line.

"There's someone who wants to talk to you," Joey said.

"Your sister."

To her astonishment, Pat LeRoy, who, along with her brother, was abandoned by her parents, ended her decades-long search for her folks.

"TIMES WERE tough, times were hard," Mrs. LeRoy says.

It was 1932, and the Great Depression had begun.

Pat, then about 1½, and her 7-month-old brother, Michael, were the children of Earl William Harper and his wife, Evelyn. Living in the Midwest, the couple realized they couldn't make a go of it there and headed south.

They arrived in Shreveport, La., in December and were unable to find jobs. By then, the couple's savings were depleted and food was scarce.

The Harper babies were malnourished and becoming more unhealthy.

Their parents took them to Shreveport's Juvenile Court, where they pleaded for assistance, according to Mrs. LeRoy.

She says she has since learned that her father told the judge, "I just cannot beg anymore."

Offering to make a contribution from his own wallet, the judge replied that his hands were otherwise tied. Because the couple legally were residents outside his jurisdiction, the court's

(See Sister found on 8A)

Scribe Adopts Baby

Clint Sanders, 24, unmarried Shreveport, La., reporter, has adopted the four months' old baby boy shown in his arms. He found the child deserted in Shreveport Juvenile court which is part of his daily 'run.' (Associated Press Photo)

Old newspaper clipping describes adoption of brother Michael

News Argus/JOHN COLLINS

Mrs. LeRoy treasurers necklace from her mother

Sister found

(Continued from 1A)

parish could not take in the children as the Harpers had hoped.

Earl and Evelyn Harper did what Mrs. LeRoy claims was their only alternative — an unthinkable choice for many people. The only way the courts could make the children their wards was if the babies' parents deserted them.

"My parents slipped out of the courtroom and left my brother and me asleep on the bench," Mrs. LeRoy says.

They never came back.

"A MICHIGAN couple, whose two infant, undernourished children were not legally entitled to receive the care and attention of the Caddo parish juvenile court, made certain Wednesday that laws of man would not deprive the tots of a livelihood," a newspaper reported. "They carried both children into the reception room of the court and abandoned them."

The word "abandon" flows uneasily over the lips of Pat LeRoy today. She, too, describes her parents' flight just as the reporter did, but nearly in tears and with a racing voice.

It did not take long for Louisiana court officials to realize they had been left holding two children without parents. Decisions had to be made regarding the youngsters' placement.

Mrs. LeRoy and her sibling went separate ways.

Pat, whose parents left her with a gold Christian medal around her neck that she still wears, was sent to Juvenile Hall. She remained there briefly until she was adopted by Joseph and Elizabeth Jouett, the owners of a Shreveport grocery store.

Referring to them as "Mama" and "Daddy," Mrs. LeRoy says, "I was very blessed. I had Christian parents and a granny."

Michael did not have to go to Juvenile Hall with his sister. He was adopted on the spot by a 24-year-old, unmarried newspaper reporter, Clinton Sanders. His care of the infant made headlines across the country as wire services picked up the story from the Shreveport newspapers.

"Its essence was such as to touch the very heartstrings of the American people," one writer commented on the story.

"When Clinton Sanders walked into the juvenile court room last December and saw the helpless babe, deserted by parents who could not support it, he decided something should be done," recounted a 1933 article. "He phoned his mother, made the arrangements and took the baby home and thought the matter was ended."

It wasn't.

Three days later, tiny Michael Harper — starving and suffering from numerous maladies — died, resulting in another round of blaring headlines.

LIFE CONTINUED for young Pat Jouett. Growing up in Shreveport, she had a happy childhood with her adoptive parents, she remembers. Mrs. LeRoy says she was particularly fond of her grandmother, Nellie Williams Reese, who helped raise her.

Her idyllic life was temporarily shattered when "a nosy neighbor" unceremoniously informed her at age 8 that Pat was adopted.

The Jouetts confirmed this, but stressed to Pat that she "was loved and wanted." Reassured, Pat put the issue behind her, yet thoughts of her biological family remained, she says.

Jouett sold his grocery store, retired and moved his family to Arkansas. There, Mrs. LeRoy met Ronald Goss, whom she married at 18. The couple had three children — Mickey, Beth and Joey.

By then, Mrs. LeRoy says, curiosity about her natural parents got the best of her, and she cautiously broached the subject with the Jouetts. She told them she wanted to locate the Harpers.

"I thought it might hurt Mama and Daddy's feelings," she recalls, "but they said no, to go ahead. I had no idea how to go about looking or anything."

Her initial inquiries did not yield any results, and the years passed. Mrs. LeRoy and her husband divorced. She later married Henry Philip LeRoy, with whom she had four additional children.

The family was sent to Okinawa while LeRoy served in the U.S. Air Force. Upon their return in 1972, the LeRoys remained in Goldsboro.

Again, Mrs. LeRoy set out to find her parents. Louisiana Juvenile Court officials informed her that her adoption file was sealed.

Stymied, Mrs. LeRoy says, her search ground almost to a halt until her daughter, Doricia Benton, contacted the Louisiana officials on her mother's behalf last March.

Again, the response was the same — Mrs. Benton and Mrs. LeRoy could not study the adoption file without permission from a judge. This time, Mrs. LeRoy pushed the matter, and a Juvenile Court judge finally relented. The records were unsealed and mailed to Mrs. LeRoy.

And they contained a surprise.

DIVING INTO the documents, Mrs. LeRoy came across a name she didn't recognize — Gertrude. Upon careful reading, she understood her discovery.

"I said, 'My goodness! I've got a sister I didn't know I had.'"

Evelyn Harper was either already pregnant or about to conceive when she and Earl Harper abandoned their firstborns in Louisiana. The couple kept Gertrude and, Mrs. LeRoy has just learned, had other children as well.

Harper had died in 1971, followed by his widow in 1990. "I just hated that so bad," Mrs. LeRoy says, adding she very much wanted to meet her parents and understand their actions.

This left a sister to find, and Mrs. LeRoy and her children — invigorated by their new information — set out on a quest.

Social Security was unable to assist in finding Gertrude, and numerous other tactics failed as well, Mrs. LeRoy says. Her son, Joey, became "my greatest private detective" and "kept calling and writing and going everywhere" for his mother.

Early this month, the years of looking finally paid off when Joey Goss discovered Gertrude Lovell in a small town outside Seattle. Confirming her identity, he persuaded her to join him in the three-way phone call to her sister Pat at the school.

"Shocked" and "stunned," are two adjectives Mrs. LeRoy uses to describe her reaction to that phone call. "I went all to pieces. Both of us were crying."

In several conversations since then, Mrs. LeRoy has gleaned from Mrs. Lovell a few facts about her family. "She said my mother talked about me all the time and that she has always known about me."

Evelyn Harper was hopeful that her abandoned child would be found, Mrs. Lovell told Mrs. LeRoy. Mrs. Harper gave a nephew of Mrs. Lovell's a necklace and told him, "When you find Patricia Frances, give this to her."

Mrs. LeRoy received the jewelry in the mail and says she treasures it.

She leaves Monday for a two-week visit to her sister's in Seattle. Her round-trip airline ticket was given to her by the staff of Carver Heights. "That's an awfully nice gift to give someone."

Mrs. LeRoy also has begun looking for two brothers Mrs. Lovell told her exist but with whom Gertrude has lost contact. When asked why her sister did not know their brothers' whereabouts, she responded with a statement that could apply to much of her own life.

"I don't know why."

It's Your Sister

Goldsboro
News-Argus

Vol: 107—No. 85   P.O. Box 10629 — Goldsboro, N.C. 27532   July 15, 1993

Reunion with sister 'like dream come true'

By LYNN WOOTEN
News-Argus Staff Writer

"I was very excited and a whole lot nervous about meeting my sister for the first time.... It was like a dream come true."

That is how Pat LeRoy summed up her encounter with her long-lost sister, whom she visited in Seattle last month.

Last month, the News-Argus reported how Mrs. LeRoy and her baby brother Michael, had been abandoned by their destitute parents in a courtroom in Shreveport, La., during the Great Depression.

Michael was adopted by a reporter when he was discovered abandoned. The baby died a few days later from exposure and malnourishment.

Mrs. LeRoy was adopted and raised by a Louisiana couple and has sought her roots for several decades.

Years of inquiry yielded information that her parents had given birth to a daughter and two sons after leaving their firstborns asleep in the Shreveport courtroom.

Mrs. LeRoy's years of searching ended early in June when her son helped her locate her sister, Gertrude Lovell, in Seattle.

The staff of Carver Heights Elementary School, where Mrs. LeRoy works, gave her a round-trip airline ticket to Seattle so she could meet her sister.

Mrs. LeRoy was met at the airport by Mrs. Lovell's nephew, Jerry, who "explained that Gertrude was just

Mrs. LeRoy, left, with sister, Mrs. Lovell, in Seattle

(See Reunion on 12A)

Reunion

(Continued from 1A)

too excited and nervous to come to the airport," she said.

"When we got to her house, she was opening the car door before I could get out, and we were crying and hugging each other," she added.

The women poured over photo albums and discussed their lives. "She told me lots of stories about all of our family," Mrs. LeRoy said. "I was trying to remember everything she told me. A lifetime of stories is hard to remember."

The visit also included Mrs. LeRoy meeting her natural mother's oldest living brother and a visit to the cemetery where her mother is buried.

"We both wished our mother could have lived to see our reunion," Mrs. Leroy said.

After two weeks of catching up, it was time for Mrs. LeRoy to return to Goldsboro. "Saying goodbye was so much harder than saying hello," she said. "It was very, very emotional for us, with a promise to always stay in touch and to see each other soon."

Left and Found

Chapter Nine

A Wish Come True

We always had an end of school luncheon the last day of school before summer vacation. Unknown to me, my co-workers at Carver Heights were planning a surprise for me. What a surprise! They knew I wanted to go to Seattle and meet Gertrude. It was hard for me to realize that I had had a sister for 60 years, and had found her and was planning a trip as soon as possible to meet her. At our end of school luncheon, my co-workers gave me a beautiful card with a box of airsickness pills so I could enjoy my flight to Seattle. Can you believe this? They presented me with $500 to pay for my airline ticket to Seattle. I was caught so by surprise, I started to cry and could not stop. I thanked them, thanked them and still could not stop crying. One of my friends said, "Pat, that $500 is going to get you to Seattle, but how are you going to get back?" It was funny of her to say that, and we all had a good laugh. What can I say about wonderful friends like that? What I said was "I will never forget what you have done for me and I love you all." Do not let anyone tell you that women cannot keep a secret. I personally know of 90 women who did it.

When I talked to Gertrude at school that Thursday, there were only five days left until school was out. 'There had been several sad things happen to our school family that year, so when Gertrude and I found each other after 60 years, it was a happy thing for all of us. My friend Jane Walston, who taught across the hall from our classroom, decided to ask our co-workers to help buy my airline ticket to meet my sister Gertrude. I am sure it was not easy to keep something like that a secret, but she did a first class job. Thank you, Jane. I will never forget what you did for me. When I called Phil, my husband, to tell him what my friends had done for me, he just could not believe it.

Time flew as I became more and more excited about my trip to Seattle to meet my sister. I have never been afraid to fly so the plane trip was not a problem. My flight was at 7:15 a.m. from Raleigh-Durham Airport on US Airways. I was up at 4 a.m. to be sure I did not miss it. I was very excited and a whole lot nervous about meeting my sister for the first time. The flight to Seattle was great. I was telling people near me on the plane about finding my sister, and even though these people did not know me, they were happy for me. I guess they could tell how excited and happy I was. As we neared Seattle, I became a bit nervous. After all, I was going clear across the United States to meet a sister I did not know I had until two weeks earlier. As we landed, I said a prayer of thanks to God for a safe trip. After I got off the plane, I was looking around for Gertrude's nephew. She had told me that he would be at the airport to meet me. I did not know what he looked like. Then this tall, handsome man walked to me. He asked me if I was Pat. I said, "Yes, how did you know?" He said he knew who I was because he had called Phil and he had told him what I was wearing and that I had a movie camera with me, along with everything else I was carrying. He was so nice that I felt right at ease. I was looking for Gertrude and asked if she was at the airport too. He said Gertrude was just too nervous and

Left and Found

Top Secret!!

Dear Carver Heights family,

A miracle has occurred within our staff. Our dear friend, Pat LeRoy, has just found a sister! She discovered about a month ago that she had a sister somewhere and has searched everywhere for her. She received a phone call here at school last Thursday at 11:30 AM. Her son had found the sister in Seattle, Washington and they were both on the phone. Pat and Gertrude desperately want to meet each other in person as soon as possible. Is it possible that we could help Pat buy a plane ticket? We all know that Pat has a generous and loving heart. If everybody in the building contributed $5.00, we would almost have the $550 she needs for a plane ticket. Of course, more or less would be greatly appreciated. Maybe we could present our gift to her at our luncheon on Thursday. We've had so many tragedies this year and we've all helped those people. Now

let's help someone celebrate a happy occasion. Pat does not know about this so keep it quiet! Thank you!

Pat's friend,
Jane W.

and excited to come to the airport, but she sure was waiting for me to get to her house. We went to get the rest of my luggage and soon we were on the way to Gertrude's house. Her nephew had a car phone and he put a call through to Phil, I spoke briefly to him to let him know I was in Seattle and we were on our way to Gertrude's house.

Seattle was so big and beautiful. I never saw so much traffic! I sure was glad I was not driving. Gertrude's nephew was pointing out so many things and I was trying to look at everything and remember all that he was telling me. It was about a 30-mile drive to Everett from Seattle. The he said, "We are almost there Pat." Now, I really got nervous, but my excitement was a stronger emotion. When we pulled into Gertrude's driveway, she was at my car door before I could open it. We were hugging and talking and hugging. Gertrude was crying and I was beside myself with happiness. It was very emotional for both of us. It was like a wish come true. I really wanted to believe that our mother knew we had found each other after all these years. How I wished our mother could have been there to share that moment. Then I met Cal, Gertrude's very dear friend, and her son Larry and his daughter Kelly. Later I met her other children, Reesa and Eddie. She has such a sweet family. Everyone was so nice to me. I knew in my heart that I would always remember this trip. We all went inside because even in June it is cool in Washington. Cal even had a fire in the fireplace and it sure felt good.

Gertrude and I sat on the couch, and talked and talked and looked and looked at pictures. We were having a wonderful time in our own little world. Gertrude gave me lots of pictures of our mother and father and some pictures of me when I was a baby. These pictures are so special to me. She said, "Pat, I have always known about you and Michael." We talked some more, I mean some more, because we

Left and Found

wanted to know everything about each other. I said, "Gertrude, you go first. I want to know all about our family history. I just want to know everything." Well, Gertrude said, "Our grandfather, Michael Joseph McCauley, II, was born in Slige, Ireland, January 26, 1889. He came to America when he was 16 years old. He died of pneumonia in September 1928. He was 39 years old. Gertrude said our grandfather was Irish Catholic and loved corned beef and cabbage once a week. He spoke proper English and was a strict disciplinarian. He was a steamfitter by trade.

Our mother Evelyn and our grandfather Michael Joseph McCauley

Our mother always said our grandmother, Nellie Mae Stevens, was quite a character! She was born in Lawrence, Illinois, on June 24, 1890. Grandmother died June 14, 1953; she was 62 years old.

Gertrude told me so many stories about our family and I shared pictures too. I was trying to remember everything she was telling me, but a lifetime of stories is hard to remember. We stayed up late talking and I soon discovered there was a three-hour difference in time. I did not have jet lag but time lag! We talked and shared stories the whole two and a half weeks I was there. By the time I left to go home, we felt as if we had known each other all our lives. We crammed as much as we could in those wonderful two and a half weeks. Grandmother had six children, our mother Evelyn Theresa, and five sons: Michael Joseph McCauley III, Neil Ade, Ralph Albert, Terence Dennis, and Lawrence. Our mother's only living brother, Uncle Ralph McCauley was 83 years old. Next, we got to our father and mother. Gertrude said our father, Earl William Harper, was born in Indianapolis, Indiana, June 16, 1900, and he died April 21, 1971. He served in the Army during World War I. He had one sister, Gertrude, and one brother, Ralph. Our father and mother had five children. Gertrude said, "You are the oldest Pat, then Michael Earl, Gertrude Evelyn, Marita Ann, Richard Floyd, and David James. Michael and Marita had died; I do not know where my two brothers, Richard and David, are. I have not known for years. We have tried to find them on the computer."

I was thinking to myself, "Where are Richard and David?"

Then we started talking about our mother. We laughed and cried as we talked about the special things she enjoyed. I just could not believe how many interests we both shared. She loved to write long informative letters and to read and write short stories and poems. She loved to talk to people and to have company. These were the exact same things I loved to do. My mother loved flowers and animals too. Gertrude told me she grew beautiful flowers inside and outside her trailer home. There was one thing my mother and I did not share: The last twenty years she lived, she hardly went outside their trailer home.

"Gertrude's"

PICTURES

Gertrude and our brother Sonny

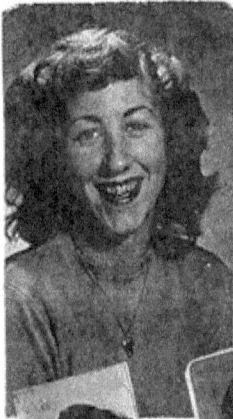

Our mother
Evelyn and
her dog. She
loved Animals
and flowers.

Pictures of
our mother
when she was
Older.

only piece
of my
birth Certificate
my mother had
when she
passed
away

This picture was made in Hot Springs Arkansas (Aug. 1932)

This picture was made in Hot Springs Arkansas (Aug. 1932)

Our mother and father at River View Park. (Aug. 1932)

Our father, Earl William Hayser (left) and one of his World War one buddies.

Our mother, Evelyn and my father Earl at the River View Park in Chicago (Aug. 1932)

Patsy riding a mule at River View Park in Chicago (Aug. 1932)

Gertrude told me our mother had a little address book and on June 2 she wrote my birthday. Gertrude went on to say, "Our mother loved her family and did the best she could for them. She was not well and would not see a doctor about her health problems or an eye doctor either. She was just very firm about that decision." I could not understand this, and was thinking, "If only she would have seen a doctor, perhaps I would have gotten to see her." Nevertheless, I have to accept that it was just not meant to be. I know that God makes no mistakes and I live with that belief.

Our mother called me Patsy and so did my adoptive mama and daddy. Our mother called Michael, "Mickie." Isn't that something? I call my Michael "Mickie" too; he is my oldest son. Gertrude said when she was 6 years old, our father and mother separated. He was not dependable or reliable to watch us, children. He was not allowed to live with his family because of his drinking and abuse. Mrs. Scarfield, our landlady, watched us and kept our father away, but sometimes he was good to us. Gertrude said she remembered living in Chicago as being good. She said she had good memories about things like the organ grinder and his monkey, homemade hot tamales on a pushcart, and the ragman singing a little song as he walked along. The scissor sharpener man also sang a little song as he walked. They lived in a small flat on the first floor of their apartment building. In the summer time, the weather was very hot; even the nights were hot. And they would sit up late, sometimes very late, waiting for it to be cool enough to sleep. "Our mother spent as much time as she could with us," Gertrude said. She would take us to the Brookfield Zoo, the Observatory, and the museum. One time we went to Lincoln Park, rented a boat, and rode the lagoon. We rode an inboard. One day our mother cashed in her War Bonds and took us kids to Riverside all day and most of the night. We went a couple of times to the Forest Preserve; we picked violets for our mother. Living in Chicago made you "careful for the rest of your life." Then Gertrude said, "I went to Brown School and to St. Paul's Church day school. During this time, it was 1945. Our mother had decided to leave our father and was working two jobs to save enough money to go to Lynnwood, Washington, where Grandma McCauley lived. She knew it would be a long bus ride to Seattle and then they would have to take another bus to Grandma McCauley's. Then Gertrude said, "I remember when I graduated from the eighth grade; I was 14 years old. Our mother had everything we were taking ready. We left at one o'clock in the morning on a bus for Seattle. I remember it being a long and tiring trip. Grandma McCauley had rabbits and a cow that was playful. She had beautiful sweet peas and a small garden.

Times were hard, but we loved living with our grandma. Life had really been rough for her after grandfather died so young. She had to raise six children by herself. Gertrude said Grandma did the best she could in those days. Now how about this? Grandma McCauley's name was Nellie May, and my adopted granny's name was Nellie Eleanor. Both names were Nellie. There are so many coincidences in Gertrude and my story. Our mother married John Knowles in 1965, and they were together when she died in 1990. My mother died of congestive heart failure. She had worked at Boeing Aircraft for many years before she retired. We had come across an old picture of our mother when she had worked at Boeing. I told Gertrude it was a good picture of our mother and her co-workers. Goodness Gertrude had so many pictures; it took us hours to go through them. Talk about a stroll down memory lane! Our Uncle Ralph McCauley was so nice, had quite a sense of humor. You just never knew what he was going to say. It was great to meet him and spend some time with him. Gertrude, Uncle Ralph, and I went to Evergreen Cemetery where our mother is buried. We knew how she loved flowers and we took beautiful carnations to put on her grave. Then we went to Bothell Cemetery where Grandma McCauley and Aunt Effie Jane are buried. Gertrude told me that our mother never got over leaving Michael and me in Shreveport, Louisiana. As she got older, she talked about it a lot, and she seemed to live more and more in the past. Gertrude said she talked and lived those days over and over again. I told Gertrude I was so sorry that it was that way for her. I just wish I could have told her I understood and I loved her, but as I have said before that was not to be.

We continued to talk about our mother and looked at more pictures. I was so happy about all the pictures Gertrude shared with me. I tell you she could not have been sweeter to her family or me either. Everyone just went out of his or her way to be so kind and sweet to me; I thought to myself, "This is just wonderful!"

Chapter Ten

Family Life

I told Gertrude, "I want to know all about you and your family, and then I will tell you all about me and my family. Ok?" She replied,"Ok." Gertrude married Reese Bowen Lovell in 1951. They had four children. David Reese was born first. He died in 1978 when a police car doing 90 miles per hour on a high-speed chase, with no siren just flashing lights, hit him, as he was crossing the road on his way home. Another car then hit him. He left a wife Vickie, and two children, David and Shawna. Then there is Larry Michael. He and his wife Kimberly have one daughter, Kelly. In addition, Reesa Kay was born next; then Edward Allen was born. Gertrude said she and Reese divorced in 1977. He died in 1978 of congestive heart failure. She told me she had a very special friend named Calvin Rosendahl, but she called him Cal; he was always there for her. Gertrude said she and Cal liked to go snowmobiling. They lived in Northern Washington State. In the winter, it really snowed in the mountains and was perfect for snowmobiling. They had friends who loved to go snowmobiling and they went together as a group. As Gertrude was telling me about making trails in the snow so it would seem safe and bundling up for the ride, it sounded like it would be so exciting. I was thinking maybe one day I could come back and go snowmobiling with them. Their snowmobiles were so pretty; Gertrude let me sit on hers. I wished for some snow but not too likely as it was June! Cal knew a lot about engines and kept the snowmobiles in tiptop shape. He also had built a great log splitter to cut logs for the fireplace. I told Gertrude I had to admit, with her, Cal was very nice, and he was very dependable. I had a wonderful visit; I just could not believe it. It was just like a dream come true.

"Well Pat, it is your turn now," Gertrude said. I said, "You know I sent you copies of the papers the judge sent me, so you already know about Michael and me being abandoned in the Courtroom in Shreveport, Louisiana. In addition, I sent you copies of the original stories and the picture of baby Michael and Clint Sanders. So I will start where I remember and what I was told. All right?

When mama and daddy adopted me, I was still taking a bottle. They did not have a baby bed and used a swing for my baby bed, and a coke bottle for my bottle. I loved to play in the grocery store. Sometimes the Campbell Soup Company would come and make a big pot of tomato soup and serve it to the customers in little paper cups. Also, the Wonder Bread Company would bring little loaves of Wonder Bread to give to the customers. Mama would get beautiful glass cake plates with the candy she bought. I had one for years until it was broken. I remember a fountain pen that came with a jar of peanut butter. Christmas was so special. I can remember the smell of real Christmas trees, the wooden boxes filled with candied green and red cherries, and the ribbon candy and filled candies like those that we buy in fancy tins today. Memories are wonderful, aren't they, Gertrude? I remember this incident very well! One time mama brought home some fresh pineapple, and she made some wine with them. She hid the wine in some bottles under the staircase. One day a friend of mine came over after school. We were playing house and I thought it would be fun to have a tea party. I got into mama's wine under the staircase and poured a little glass for both of us. To my great dismay, mama found out and asked me if I had gotten into the wine. I said no mama and she asked me again and I said no. Then she told me a little bird told her yes that I had gotten into the wine. That little bird was my granny. It was to my great dismay that mama found out. She gave me a spanking to remember. She said, "Look in the corner Patsy and tell me what you see." I said, "Mama I don't see anything." "Look again Patsy and tell me what you see," I said, "I still don't see anything, mama." She told me the devil was over in the corner laughing when I got a spanking because I had not told the truth. I have never forgotten that!

When Daddy would stay to check his books, I would always play in the store. Sometimes I would call my friend, Kenneth Wagstaff, who lived across the street from the store. He would come over and we would play hide and seek. I wonder where Kenneth is now. That was about 58 years ago. When mama and daddy got older, because of their health, they sold the store and retired. I believe they always missed the store. I guess I miss daddy's store too because I do not know anyone who loves to go to the grocery store and just shop as much as I do! I loved going with Daddy to take groceries to the Juvenile Home and to the jail. Everywhere he went, I, wanted to go. I guess I was like a little shadow. Daddy used to tease me and say he could have retired a millionaire if I had not eaten all his profit in candy. I knew he was just teasing me.

There was a big hill across from the grocery store and it sure was fun to get an empty cardboard box and slide down the hill over and over again, while my granny sat and watched me. She was a wonderful, caring granny and I loved her so much. Of course, she spoiled me because I was her only grandchild. Mama spoiled me, but not like daddy and granny did. When my granny was about 16 years old, she had scarlet fever and it left her deaf. However, she always told me she did not have any problems understanding me. Granny and I spent so much time together because Mama and Daddy both worked at the grocery store they owned. I thought she was the most special granny in the world. Granny made me beautiful embroidered pinafores from Daddy's shirts when the collar was worn out. Someone would say to me, "Patsy, that is such a pretty pinafore," and I would say, "It is made from my Daddy's old shirt." Granny told me that I would say that. She was a seamstress and could sew anything. She took care of Mama and herself by sewing after mama's daddy was killed while working for the railroad. He was only 29 years old. I loved his name, Stonewall Jackson Reese.

I was remembering all the things Gertrude had told me about living in Chicago. We both grew up in a big city. There was a hot tamale man too with a little cart and the hot tamales, which were wrapped in cornhusks and so very good. I remember the Louisiana State Fair; it was huge. When Huey P. Long was running for Governor of Louisiana, we went to a barbecue for him; there were lots of music and people, but it was fun. Every Saturday my Granny would take me to see a movie. My favorites were cowboy movies with Gene Aunty, Hopalong Cassidy, and Roy Rogers. After Mama and Daddy sold their grocery store and retired, we moved to Hatfield, Arkansas. It was a little town of 230 people. Everybody knew everybody. Some of my happiest memories are about Hatfield. Daddy bought a 20-acre farm with a house on it. There was no electricity or running water, and the bathroom was an old-fashioned outhouse. It was quite different from city life! We had Aladdin lamps to fill with oil; we drew all our water from the well and cut wood for the stove to cook. We had a big coal heater in the living room, but you know what, we had more time to enjoy life, than with all the modern conveniences that we have today. It was a more laid-back kind of life. There was just more time to relax and enjoy everything. It seems like today our lives are a rush! Rush! And hurry! Hurry! Not much time to stop and smell the roses anymore and that is very sad, isn't it?

I loved going to a country school. It was only one brick building with downstairs for elementary school and upstairs for the Hatfield High School. There were friendships made that would endure a lifetime. Some of my best memories are of those special years. All too soon, those years were gone and we graduated and would go on to the next phase in our lives. Think about it, how quickly we went from a baby to childhood to adolescence to an adult. We need to treasure each day. Let me tell you about one of my special memories of living in Hatfield. Since daddy had bought a small farm, he felt he should have some farm animals. Well, we had always raised goats even when we lived in Shreveport. Daddy believed that goat's milk was healthier for you to drink than cow's milk. One time in Shreveport the nanny goat got out of the back yard and chewed a couple of shirts off of the clothesline next door. Daddy had to replace the shirts. By the way, goats also eat the paper off the tin cans. He also bought us a cow, horse, some chickens, a rooster, and a pig. Not long after daddy bought his farm, the Health Department told him to re-drill the well because the family that lived there before us had contracted typhoid fever from the water. Of course, daddy made quick arrangements to have the well re-drilled so we could drink the water. The workers must have left the cover off the well and suddenly we heard a "Baa, Baa, blub, blub," and we ran out into the yard and again we heard, "Baa, baa, blub, blub." It sounded like it was coming from the well. When we looked down into the well, there was Daddy's favorite nanny goat bobbing up and down in the water, and still going baa, baa, blub, blub. By this time Daddy had gotten a long rope; he tied it around himself and told Mama and me to lower him down into the well. We did and he tied the rope around the nanny goat that was still going baa, baa, blub, blub. Daddy then told us to pull her up. It was not easy as she was kicking, and she was so scared. We finally got her to the top and she was okay. Then we dropped the rope back to daddy and he tied it around himself again, and we pulled him up. It was not easy pulling Daddy up, but soon he was at the top of the well and he was all right. What an experience and a priceless memory for me.

I was in eleventh grade when we moved from Hatfield to Mena, Arkansas, which was the County Seat. I finished high school at Mena in 1949. Although I graduated from Mena High, my heart was still with my classmates at Hatfield. When I go to Hatfield class reunions, everyone makes me feel that I am still part of "our class." It is always wonderful to see old friends and to recall the best of memories. We are all still very good friends and keep in touch with each other. When we were all in high school, who was thinking about our 50th Class reunion? Not us! We were too busy just being teenagers. In fact, in 1999, we celebrated our 50th class reunion. After we had moved to Mena, I met a nice young man. His name was Ronald Ellis Goss, and we fell in love and married June 3, 1949. I was 18 the day before. In 1950, he was sent to Korea with the National Guard Unit from Mena and was gone for a year. When Ronnie came home, we moved to Little Rock, Arkansas, where he enrolled in a school for TV and worked at a local TV station. We had three children: Ronald Michael, M. Elizabeth, and Joseph Ellis. We were married seven years and were divorced in 1956. Mickie, BeBe, Joey, and I stayed in Little Rock, Arkansas. About a year later, I met a Staff Sergeant stationed at Little Rock AFB. He was nice and I liked him a lot. His name was Henry Philip LeRoy. We went together for 3 months, and we were married November 29, 1957. We have four children: Philip Kevin, Lucinda Louise, Patrick Shannon, and Doricia Shawnee. I have 7 children, 14 grandchildren, and 15 great-grandchildren. Now that is a good size family, wouldn't you think? After Phil and I had been married, he was sent on temporary duty to Shreveport, Louisiana, for 3 weeks. The children and I went to spend a few days with him. The Air Force was forming a new MMS Squadron at Seymour Johnson Air Force Base, Goldsboro, North Carolina. He had already received his PCS orders to be a part of the new squadron. When your husband is in the military, you move a lot, sometimes to other states and sometimes to other countries. When we got to Goldsboro, there were no houses to rent, so we bought a new home and settled in. We enjoyed the small town living.

About five years later Philip received PCS orders for Naha AFB in Okinawa. Now this would really be a new experience for all of us. I had quite a time getting my passport. Even though I had a copy of my birth certificate, I did not have a copy of my adoption papers. A call to my adopted mama and daddy soon straightened everything out. They were living in Mena, Arkansas, since they had sold their grocery store and retired. It was 300 miles round trip to Shreveport, Louisiana. The next day my parents drove to Shreveport to get me a true and certified copy of my adoption papers. Then they sent the papers to me so I would be able to get my passport. Again, I deeply appreciated my adoptive parents; all my life they had been right there for me. I knew I could count on them no matter the situation. Soon all the required papers were in order as well as all of the required shots to be able to travel abroad. Then we were on our way to Okinawa! Mama and Daddy were getting old now and I knew it worried them that I was going so far away. However, they did not say a word. They just wished us safe travel and let us go with love and their blessings. I know they prayed for us every day until they knew we were safe in Okinawa. I remember growing up in a home where every morning we held hands at breakfast and had prayer. I was so blessed to grow up in a Christian home with so much love. We were stationed first at Naha AFB, and then Philip was transferred to Kadena AFB, still in Okinawa. Okinawa is not big; it is 75 miles long and 25 miles wide at its widest part. Some of my best ever memories are in two tours we spent in Okinawa; altogether, we were there about 5 and a half years. Many years before, Mama had given me my baby book and all the original newspaper stories about Michael and me. She also gave me a paper with my father's brother and sister's names on it. I wanted to find them but did not know how. Nor did I know how to go about finding my birth parents either. While we were in Okinawa, I became very sick and wondered if I would even live long enough to come home. Still I kept alive the hope that one day I would find my birth parents.

We returned home from Okinawa in February 1972. We went by Shreveport to see Sue Bell, my adoptive father's daughter. We also stopped by the cemetery to say "good-by" to my daddy who had passed away in December 1971, and Mama, and Granny, who were buried there. It was very emotional. On an impulse I said, "Philip, can we go by Juvenile Hall and let me ask about my birth parents?" I stepped up to the information desk and explained to the woman who I was and what I would like to know about my parents. She said, "Wait right here, please." She opened a door, stood there a moment or so, then stepped inside, as the door slowly closed behind her. In a little while, she returned with a firsthand report. She was holding a folder, yellowed with age. Written on the corner was "Patricia and Michael Harper." She would not let me see the paper inside the folder. However, she did read me a letter my birth mother had written many years before asking about Michael and me. Then she wrote down the names of my father's brother and sister. These were the same names my adoptive mama had given me years before. These were the first names I asked the telephone operator to locate for me. I still have these names even though I was unable to find them. The woman looked at me and said, "Honey' don't try to find them; leave well enough alone." I knew in my heart that I would not give up trying to find my birth parents; I felt I just had to tell them I loved them and I understood. Give up hope? I could not; I just could not! It was my hope that kept me searching. It seemed no matter how I tried, I could not find the information I needed to find my birth parents. It certainly was not because I was not trying! After Doricia contacted the judge, and he opened the records that been sealed for so many years, I began to hope again. I wanted so very desperately to believe that there was a chance to find my birth parents. Talk about excited! Was I ever? I was so happy to share everything I had found in the records with you. Of course, the rest is history—of how Joey found you. Now here we are talking, laughing, and getting to know each other." I stayed two and a half weeks, but wished I had stayed longer, not realizing how special and precious those days would be!

Mama Daddy
and Patsy beside
Daddy's Grocery
Store—

Granny and
Patsy in front
of Daddy's
Grocery Store.

Mama, Granny
and Patsy

Patsy's
Pictures

Patsy and her doll in front of her daddy's store. She still has the doll.

Patsy at 18

PET WINNERS TO GET PRIZES

More Than 100 Animals Are Paraded by Masters on City Streets

Shreveport citizens thronged the downtown streets yesterday to see the annual Shreveport Optimist Mascot parade with its more than 100 entries of pets of all kinds and their masters.

Winners of the pet parade will be awarded their prizes at Monday night's ball game where they will be guests of the Sports baseball team.

One of the winners, Mary Alice Roberson, 11, of 1432 Arlington avenue, stopped to pick up her pet dog during the parade and a truck following right behind her was unable to stop and ran over her foot. She was rushed to the Charity hospital by I. L. Smith, of 1427 Arlington avenue, where an X-ray showed that no bones were broken. Mary suffered only bruises and was returned to her home, hospital attendants said.

Winners in the various classifications are as follows:

MOST UNIQUE MASCOT: First, Merritt Boydston, Jimmy Rosenbloom and Jack Kaplan, 544 Slattery boulevard; second, Billy King, 4901 Mansfield road; third, Paula Tuquille; fourth, Bobby June Harper, 4051 Velva street.

BEST DRESSED MASCOT: First, Bobby Sheppard, 3115 Judson street; second, Elsie Joyce Smith, 3117 Judson street; third, Bruce Garrett, 2618 Marion street; fourth, Leon Thornton, 1601 Howard street.

BEST TRAINED TRICK MASCOT: First, Warren Eason, 2413 James street; second, Marjie Hilton, 913 Spring street.

SMALLEST DOG: First, Gloria Foster, 302 Quinton street; second, Billy Ray Roberts, 534 Riverside drive; third, Anthony Todro, 2215 Darien street.

LARGEST DOG: First, Louis McRaynolds, 317 East 68th street.

TAMEST MASCOT: Helen Ann Roberts, 2411 Southern avenue.

WILDEST MASCOT (lion): Robert Ricord.

BEST MANNERED HORSE: Two fine horses were entered and won prizes, but names were not secured; third, Ray Kightlinger, Shetland pony.

DRESSED TO MATCH: Mary Alice Roberson, 1432 Arlington street (dog and girl dressed alike).

THREE OF A KIND: Triplet goats, Patsy Jouett, 1087 Louisiana avenue.

Pets of Shreveport children were on parade here yesterday in downtown Shreveport and Patsy Jouett, 1087 Louisiana avenue, (at top) turns around to see how her prize-winning triplet goats are coming along. BELOW—the young lady seems to be having a bit of trouble with her tiny pet. Evidently "Nanny" sees someone she knows among the throng on Texas street. The picture shows part of the parade as it passed on Texas street. (Times Photo.)

110   Left and Found

Chapter Eleven

Farewell Gertie

After I had returned home, Gertrude and I kept in contact via phone calls, letters, and cards. I was going to retire soon and was planning a trip to see her. This time I wanted to drive to Seattle, instead of flying. The years went by so fast and soon it had been four years since we had seen each other. I had planned my trip for the coming spring. However, that trip was not to be. A phone call changed those plans.

When I came in from work that September 30, 1997, there was a message on my answering machine. The message was brief; all it said was, "Pat this is Cal, Gertie's Cal; call me." Even though the message was short, I sensed something was wrong. Right away, I began to call and call, but I could not get an answer. This, of course, made me feel that something was very wrong. I knew Gertrude had a problem with her eyes ever since I was there. Her doctor had put her on 10 steroids a day. I could not believe that! Every time I spoke to her or wrote to her, I pleaded with her to see another doctor and to question the use of so many steroids. However, she never did, I feel sure she did not want to worry me as I was so far away. I just imagined everything since I did not know what was wrong. Finally, in desperation, I called Uncle Ralph, our mother's only living brother.

At that time, he was 83. Gertrude's son Larry answered the phone. I asked him what was wrong and told him I had a call from Cal. He said he thought I already knew what had happened. I told him I did not know anything. Then he told me Gertrude was in the hospital in critical condition. I could not believe it and just went to pieces and could not stop crying.

Larry gave me the hospital's phone number. I called the hospital and they connected me to her room. She was not able to take phone calls, but when she found out it was me, she took my call. She sounded so weak; I could hardly understand her. Gertrude said, "Pat, I only have one more day and they are going to disconnect all life support." I was crying as I said, "Gertrude, please promise you won't l let them disconnect anything! I am getting on an emergency flight to come to be with you." She promised me she would wait for me. As we talked softly, it seemed unbelievable that this impasse was happening to us. My thoughts were racing as I thought about losing Gertrude. It just was not fair, just was not fair! Before we said good-bye, we told each other how much we cared for each other and loved one another. After I hung up the phone, the flood of tears would not stop. However, I knew I had to be strong for this trip to Seattle. My son-in-law, Larry, called US Airways and made all the emergency arrangements for me. US Airways put him on hold while they checked the Seattle Hospital to be sure it was an emergency. While Larry was talking on the phone, I was packing and getting ready to go. When I arrived at the Raleigh-Durham airport, the US Airways personnel could not have been more caring or thoughtful of my situation. In addition, when I changed planes, they were just as caring and thoughtful of me too. I did then and I still appreciate their caring and concern for me. It was a long flight and I was tired when we landed at Sea-Tac airport in Seattle. However, I knew I had to be strong to stand up under the heartache I was about to face.

As I walked up the hallway from the plane, I wondered who would be meeting me. As I glanced around for a familiar face, I heard someone call my name. Kelly's mother said, "Pat we are here to meet you and take you to the hospital." Kelly is Gertrude's granddaughter. Her mother and aunt had come to meet me. They were so sweet; we left right away for the hospital. It was 12 o'clock midnight when we got there; we went directly to her room. When I walked into her room, I was amazed at how much she looked like our mother. Cal said, "Gertie wanted to take a nap before you got here so she could talk to you when you got here. Gertrude's son Eddie and his dear friend Pillar were there at her bedside. I cannot remember everything we talked about; I do remember telling her how much I loved her and I came to be with her. I was trying not to cry, but tears ran down my face as I said, "Oh Gertrude, it took me 60 years to find you and now I am losing you." She told me, "Pat I love you too." It was so hard I could hardly bear it. Cal and I stayed the night, but neither of us slept and poor Gertrude was so restless as we sat at the end of her bed. The nurse had fixed our chairs so we could sleep, but, believe me, there was no sleep for us that night. As the morning light broke through the sky, I knew this would be one of the hardest days I would have to face in my life. The best place to go when only God can ease your pain is the Hospital Chapel, which is always open. Very early Gertrude's son Larry, her daughter Reesa, and I went to the chapel and prayed quietly for their mother and my sister. We also wrote down our prayers in a book. I know and understand that God makes no mistakes, and ours is not to question "why" but to believe and accept His will in our lives.

That morning the nurses came and removed all life support except one IV directly into her chest. As the pain became more intense, the nurse gave her more medication to ease her pain and anxiety. The nurse explained to Gertrude that if she breathed through her nose and out her mouth it would be easier for her. She would do fine for a few minutes then panic. I sat in a chair right beside her head. As I glanced across her bed, I was looking right at Eddie and Pillar; I could see and feel their sadness and grief. Cal was also sitting close by and I could see the same sadness and grief. I took Gertrude's hands in mine and whispered softly repeatedly, "Breathe through your nose honey and out your mouth; that is real good, sugar." Then I would say again, "Breathe through your nose and out your mouth. You are doing great; now breathe through your nose and out your mouth, sweetheart. That is good honey; keep on breathing through your nose and out your mouth." I have no idea how long I sat beside her whispering those words repeatedly. I lost track of time. I have always heard that no matter what happens someone who is dying can hear you when you talk. I want to believe Gertrude could hear me whispering to her. As I was straightening her cover, I noticed how cold her feet and legs were. As I looked at Eddie and Pillar, I am sure they could tell by my face what was happening. We all knew we were losing her. Cal sat down beside her and took her hands in his. Soon her breathing became very shallow and then we could not hear her breathing at all. We called for the nurse and when she came, she said Gertrude was already off her monitor. I kept thinking how this could be happening. We were all crying and trying to comfort each other. It was so hard, so hard. The hospital staff was so kind to us; we thanked them for all they had done for Gertrude.

One of the nurses told me that the night before I came Gertrude had told her she was waiting for her sister, Pat. Bless her heart; she did wait for me. I just could not accept that she was gone. I had only known for two days that she was sick. I do not think I will ever get over losing her that way. I did not know until I got to Seattle that Gertrude had broken her hip, but she would not let anyone tell me. They said she did not want to worry me because I lived so far away. While she was in the hospital, Pillar told her, "You have to call Pat; she needs to know." So only at the last, did she let them call me. I would have gone right away if I had known she was sick. When she was admitted to the hospital a week before she passed away, they thought she had pneumonia, and then they thought it was the flu. However, the real problem was her heart. There was permanent damage to her heart. It was giving out and there was no way to save her. By the time they realized it was her heart, it was too late. The damage had weakened her heart muscle and it could not be repaired. I could not help but wonder if all those steroids, 10 a day for three years, had caused the irreparable damage to her heart. Gertrude had been right when I spoke to her on the phone; she did have only one more day. I am so very thankful I was able to see her and talk to her one more time. It is still hard for me to accept that she and I found each other after 60 years only to lose her like this. I love her family very much and want us to keep in contact with each other.

Gertrude wanted to be cremated and we honored her wishes in every way. We called, and then went to Evergreen Cemetery to make all the arrangements. It had been raining for several days, but the day of Gertrude's Memorial Service the sun was shining brightly. There were flowers and a picture collage of her life. Reesa read a poem in honor of her mother. Two beautiful songs were played and the Pastor spoke words of encouragement. So many friends came to help her family, to share their grief, and to bid "Gertie," as she was affectionately called, farewell. Gertrude is buried beside our mother, Evelyn McCauley Harper, and her oldest son, David Reese Lovell. I was asked to write her obituary for the newspaper. After her memorial service, we all went back to Gertrude's home. So many family and friends came and brought food and flowers. I stayed on for a week; everyone was so nice to me, but it was not the same without Gertrude. She had a special quiet way about her that I missed very much. Even though we were sisters, we had different personalities. Gertrude was very quiet and soft spoken, while, on the other hand, I talk a lot. Two different sisters, but that is okay! However, we both enjoyed talking on the phone and sending cards and letters to each other. Now my sister is gone and I miss her sweet ways so much. I started writing my story in 1967, 48 years ago. Then I found my sister Gertrude and added more to our story. However, before I could finish our story, there was a sad and tragic ending. I had envisioned where two sisters found each other after 60 years and were happy for many more years to come. I am so thankful God allowed us to have these years together and to meet each other and to love and care about each other. I will always treasure the special memories Gertrude and I shared. I want to call you by your special name.

Farewell, "Gertie," I will never forget you. Until we meet again in heaven. Always, your sister Patricia.

Left and Found

Chapter 12

Life Goes On

After Gertrude had passed away, sadness overwhelmed me. It was so hard to imagine that we would no longer be able to talk on the phone, write letters, or visit each other again. So, Gertrude and my memories became more precious than before. I always smile when I think about the day we first met. She was crying and I was laughing; hers were tears of joy and my laughing was happiness. How different we were; she was so soft-spoken and quiet and I am so outgoing and definitely not quiet! However, we hit it off right away. Oh, the many hours we talked, talked, and looked at our family pictures. I will always treasure the two years Gertrude and I had together, and I will never forget her and her family. She passed away and left me so sad. How true that life goes on no matter what situations becomes a part of our lives. I have continued with my life with a desire and passion to enjoy each day.

After I retired as a teacher assistant in 1995, I worked as a substitute teacher for Wayne County Schools. I have always loved teaching children. Then my friend Judy Morris told me about AmeriCorps and an opportunity to work for them. I filled out an application and was hired as a volunteer to work with VISTA (Volunteers in Service to America). It was a one-year contract. I had a classroom at

Vocational Rehabilitation building and worked with clients to teach them Independent living skills. This was a very rewarding experience. I also received a $1,200 bonus at the end of my first year. The second year I worked with AmeriCorps in a program called CAREERS (Consumers Achieving Real Employment Enrichment Retention Services). I had an office at social services and worked with great people and we became good friends. I worked with Work First and Welfare to work. I really enjoyed working with my clients. This was another rewarding experience in my life. I received a $4,725 Educational Award, which I put to good use at Wayne Community College. Since education is one of my many passions, this was great! At 74, I was having the time of my life. I have two more quarters I can take to use all my Education Award; I have taken English and Grammar, also humanities and creative writing classes. In my English class, I wrote a paragraph about the computer. I called the computer "Dr. Jekyll and Mr. Hide," because there are many good things to be learned, but it will also hide many things that are not good. I also took a creative writing class and learned so much about poetry. For one thing, I learned that not all poems have to rhyme. In addition, I wrote a fiction story called "The Donut Hole Caper," which was published in the Renaissance 2004 book published by Wayne Community College. I have always enjoyed writing stories and poems. The poems in this book are original poems that I wrote.

My Methodist church was very dear to my heart; it was a small neighborhood church where everyone knows each other; it was like a big Church family. I was editor of our monthly newsletter. We had a wonderful outreach ministry and a great Vacation Bible School. Once a year it is Women's Day at church and each year a different woman speaks. One year I volunteered to speak and I would like to share my angel story with you.

I was a bit nervous and maybe it is true that it is easier to speak to an audience of strangers than folks you know. That Saturday before I was to speak on Sunday at church, I had to go to the commissary on the AFB and my grandson Rance went with me to help me. While sitting in a driving grocery cart, I was watching Rance put my groceries on the checkout counter. A very pretty African-American young woman spoke to me. She said she felt led to pray for me and asked if it would be all right. I said yes it would be fine. She knelt down beside me and prayed a beautiful prayer for me. While she was praying for me, there was total silence except for her voice and you know how noisy it is in a grocery store. When she finished praying, she stood up and she seemed to disappear just as she appeared to me. It was such a strange feeling. Rance was about 3 or 4 feet away from me and I asked him if he heard the young woman praying for me. He said, "No grandma." Then I asked him if he saw the young woman kneeling by my chair. Again, he said, "No, grandma." It was a wonderful experience that I will never forget. She must have been an angel. When I spoke at church the next day, it went fine.

A couple of years ago I decided to make Barbie Doll clothes again. In the 1960's, my husband Phil was stationed with the U.S. Air Force in Okinawa. I had a sew girl, Miyoko, who made me beautiful clothes. We would go to the oriental material store and choose material; it was so hard to decide because all of the materials were gorgeous. This was when I thought it would be a great idea to make Barbie doll clothes for Cindy's doll. Soon I was selling doll clothes to my friends. I had bought one set of Barbie Doll patterns; from then on, I began to design my own original doll clothes. The next

Christmas when Santa came to the Base Exchange, Cindy asked for a new Barbie doll because her mama had taken her doll to use to make doll clothes. I was so embarrassed. The next year I put my doll clothes in the officer's gift shop. That year I made a $1,000. That was exciting! My doll clothes are still original styles and sell for more than in the 1960's. Each dress is hand finished and has stoles, purses, and hats to match. When I start making doll clothes, I just do not know when to quit because it is so enjoyable.

One year my friend Toby Heidelmeier called and asked if I would like to take painting classes at Southeastern Medical Oncology Center (SMOC), our doctor's office. It was called Soul Palette. It was started when a woman who had terminal cancer was asked by the doctor if there was something she always wanted to do; she said she always wanted to paint a picture. One of the counselors knew an artist who might be interested and contacted her. Her name is Christy and she agreed to teach a class each Thursday at SMOC. Soon others came and now there are two classes each Thursday. This is a passion I am really enjoying and look forward to each Thursday. The fellowship and support for each other are wonderful. We have lost dear friends, but their memory and beautiful pictures live on. Another of my passions was working at Saint Stephens' Soup Kitchen as a volunteer. We called ourselves the Tuesday Lunch Bunch. We cooked meals and served the clients from 11 a.m. to 12 noon, Monday through Saturday. It makes you very appreciative of what you have. Later my daughter Doricia became the director of the New Community Soup Kitchen of Goldsboro. She started as a volunteer and ended with being the Director. I am very proud of her and all her accomplishments.

Good Neighbors

Pat LeRoy's Tuesdays are spoken for

Pat LeRoy, Soup Kitchen volunteer

News-Argus/ED HAYDEN

By AMY COOK
News-Argus Staff Writer

Giving of herself and of her time is nothing new for Goldsboro resident Pat LeRoy. She has been doing that for most of her life.

When she retired from the Wayne County Schools as a teaching assistant in 1995, Mrs. LeRoy became involved with the Community Soup Kitchen at Saint Stephen's Episcopal Church.

She remembers how a friend, Nancy Thompson, talked about working at the Soup Kitchen. Mrs. LeRoy says she was intrigued by her friend's stories and wanted to get involved. For over two years, Mrs. LeRoy has volunteered at the Soup Kitchen as a cook and a server.

Barbara Berkeley, the Soup Kitchen's volunteer coordinator, says it is volunteers like Mrs. LeRoy who keep the Soup Kitchen running.

"She is just a super lady," Mrs. Berkeley says. "She does so much and she is always there for us."

Every Tuesday, Soup Kitchen patrons can enjoy Mrs. LeRoy's smile and warm

See Neighbors on 2A

Continued from 1A

personality.

"I never miss a Tuesday," she says. "My friends know not to schedule me for anything on Tuesdays, because that's where I am going to be."

Mrs. LeRoy says volunteering at the Soup Kitchen gives her a good feeling.

"When you work and you get paid for that work, it's a job," she says. "When you volunteer, you are giving with your heart and the pay you get is the good feeling that you get by helping others."

"I think everyone should try and do something so they can feel this way, too," she says.

Mrs. LeRoy brings three generations of LeRoys to the Soup Kitchen.

"My daughter and some of my grandchildren have come out and helped," she says. "The whole family likes coming here and helping."

Mrs. LeRoy has seven children, 12 grandchildren and two great-grandchildren.

Besides her work at the Soup Kitchen, Mrs. LeRoy has also taught first-aid and some sign language. She teaches a Sunday school class at her church.

She worked as a teacher's assistant for the Wayne County Schools system for 22 years. She says she especially enjoyed being around the children. During the last 18 years of her teaching assistant career, Mrs. LeRoy worked with special education students.

"That was probably the most special part of my job," she says.

Soup's on

To the editor:

What do you think when you hear, "Soups on?" Time to eat, right?

During the depression of the 1930s soup kitchens were set up to feed hungry people. Soup lines were long because so many people had lost their jobs and some had lost everything. Those first soup kitchens served soup, a drink, and sometimes a sandwich.

The tradition of the soup kitchen is still carried on and today we still feed hungry folks. There are thousands of soup kitchens throughout the United States serving well balanced and nutritious meals, like St. Stephen's Community Soup Kitchen located at 200 North James Street, in its 20th year of service. We're proud to say a meal is served every day at 11 o'clock, except Sunday.

From January 1 to December 31, 1998, there were 32,158 meals served. This represents 2,376 more meals than were served in 1997. That was a daily average of 102 meals for 1998. Christmas and Thanksgiving dinners are served with turkey and all the trimmings.

Mrs. Barbara Berkeley is volunteer coordinator for the soup kitchen and works with Tuesday's "Lunch Bunch" and other volunteers. The other days of the week, Mrs. Inge Worrell and volunteers do a great job to prepare and serve meals.

Two days a week, military volunteers from Seymour Johnson AFB staff the soup kitchen. Also, the Golden K Kiwanis Club provides a volunteer each day to count the number of people served, both adult and children.

The Soup Kitchen is not government subsidized, but is supported by the community . We always need food donations and monetary contributions.

If we helped only ourselves, we would miss the opportunity to share with others. When you give of yourself for others, it will do your heart good. We need your support.

Patricia LeRoy
St. Stephen's Community
Soup Kitchen Volunteer
Goldsboro

Left and Found

I would like to add a very important dream that I would want to fulfill. I would like to buy a monument of an angel with her wings outspread. Watching over the babies buried in Babyland. I would like it to say,

"In loving memory of my precious baby brother, Michael Earl, and all the babies in Babyland."
I Love You - Your Sister Patsy

Dear to my heart is the "Lighthouse" of Wayne County for battered and abused women. I had no personal experience of domestic violence and this made me very aware of the victims. This led me to write a poem about domestic violence. There is no excuse for domestic violence. The women come seeking emotional help as well as assistance to start their lives over again. I served on the Board of Directors for six years and as Secretary for two years. Later, I served as Chairman of the Board of Directors. I was also a volunteer at the Lighthouse. This was a very rewarding experience for me. Below is the poem I wrote about the Lighthouse.

The Beacon from the Lighthouse

I was happily married with a husband and young son and things
seemed alright;
Then he began to change and all he wanted to do was fuss and
fight!

I tried to reason why such a change had made him become this
way,
Talking to him was useless and I just didn't know what to do or
say.

Our lives became worse and he began daily to hit me and our
young son;
I was so scared and didn't know where to hide or where to run.

Then I heard about the Lighthouse and I had hope and gave them a
call;
They were so kind and understanding when my life was crumbling
and at a stall.

It's so sad when you have no one to turn to and nowhere to turn;
They work with you and teach you the things you need to learn.

Then you are able to pick up the pieces of your life once more;
And be a different person than you ever were before.

With the Lighthouse's help I begun to put my life back together;
I felt that I was worthwhile and my life was so much better.

So, no matter your situation as hopeless as it might seem;
The Lighthouse will welcome you and keep you as a team.

Patricia LeRoy

Left and Found

As I write this last part of my book, I think about all of my friends and how special they are to me. We have shared good times and bad times together. We never know what tomorrow holds for us, so it is very important to live each day with love and compassion. If there is something special, you have always wanted to do, then strive to achieve your goal. I would like to leave this thought with you, "Always do your best and love others from your heart and consider them as you would yourself."

A Little Talk with Jesus

I dreamed I had a talk with Jesus and this is what He said, "I'd like to talk to you about the life you've led."

He spoke so kind and gentle but His face I could not see, and I was overcome with humbleness and humility.

He showed me where He'd found me and where He'd brought me to, how He'd saved my lost soul and what I'd promised I would do.

When you were born, I had some special plans for the life you'd live, how you would accept Me as your Savior and your life to Me you'd give.

But your life is so busy with the demands of daily living, please stop and think about it, are you really giving?

So many souls are dying and will be lost in sin forever, you must care and witness and use all your endeavor.

Your life on this earth will be short at best, then you'll have an eternity in which to rest.

Time is fleeting by with each heartbeat that you take, you need to get things straight and work and labor for My sake.

Will you be ready to meet Me with mere a regret, or are there promises that you've not met?

You know not when I'll call you to leave this world of care, for a never ending Heaven all the saved in Christ will share.

With no tears or sadness ever where sin and strife can never enter, and real happiness in Jesus is forever.

Patricia J. LeRoy
August 1979

Contact Information

For information on ordering copies of *Left and Found* or to inquire about book discussions, book signings, etc., please contact:

Kingdom Living Publishing
P.O. Box 660
Accokeek, MD 20607
publish@kingdomlivingbooks.com

(301) 292-9010

Or visit:

www.kingdomlivingbooks.com

www.ingramcontent.com/pod-product-compliance
Lightning Source LLC
LaVergne TN
LVHW051133080426
835510LV00018B/2389